Nobel Lectures

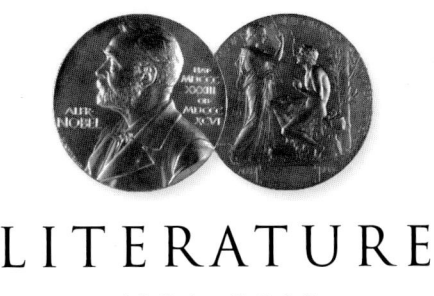

# LITERATURE
1996 – 2000

# Nobel Lectures
### Including Presentation Speeches and Laureates' Biographies

## Physics
## Chemistry
## Physiology or Medicine
## Literature
## Peace
## Economic Sciences

# Nobel Lectures
### Including Presentation Speeches and Laureates' Biographies

# LITERATURE
## 1996 – 2000

Editor

## Horace Engdahl
The Swedish Academy
Stockholm

**World Scientific**
*New Jersey • London • Singapore • Hong Kong*

*Published for the Nobel Foundation in 2002 by*
World Scientific Publishing Co. Pte. Ltd.
5 Toh Tuck Link, Singapore 596224
*USA office:* Suite 202, 1060 Main Street, River Edge, NJ 07661
*UK office:* 57 Shelton Street, Covent Garden, London WC2H 9HE

**NOBEL LECTURES IN LITERATURE (1996–2000)**

*All rights reserved.*

ISBN 981-02-4962-4
ISBN 981-238-000-0 (pbk)

Printed by FuIsland Offset Printing (S) Pte Ltd, Singapore

# FOREWORD

Since 1901 the Nobel Foundation has published annually "Les Prix Nobel" with reports from the Nobel award ceremonies in Stockholm and Oslo as well as the biographies and Nobel lectures of the laureates. In order to make the lectures available for people with special interests in the different prize fields the Foundation gave Elsevier Publishing Company the right to publish in English the lectures for 1901–1970, which were published in 1964–1972 through the following volumes:

| | |
|---|---|
| Physics 1901–1970 | 4 vols. |
| Chemistry 1901–1970 | 4 vols. |
| Physiology or Medicine 1901–1970 | 4 vols. |
| Literature 1901–1967 | 1 vol. |
| Peace 1901–1970 | 3 vols. |

Thereafter, and until the year 2000, the Nobel Foundation has given World Scientific Publishing Company the right to bring the series up to date and also publish the Prize lectures in Economics from the year 1969. The Nobel Foundation is very pleased that the intellectual and spiritual message to the world laid down in the laureates' lectures, thanks to the efforts of World Scientific, will reach new readers all over the world.

Bengt Samuelsson  
*Chairman of the Board*

Michael Sohlman  
*Executive Director*

*Stockholm, August 2001*

# PREFACE

The early volumes of the series *Nobel Lectures* were published in 1964–1972. The one covering the Prize in Literature, published in 1969, brought together all the lectures, presentation speeches and laureates' biographies for the period 1901–1967. In 1991, the Nobel Foundation decided to update the series, and two volumes covering the period 1968–1990 were published in 1993, followed in 1997 by a third volume covering the years 1991–1995, The present volume brings together all the lectures, speeches and biographies for the period 1996–2000.

Horace Engdahl
*Permanent Secretary of the Swedish Academy*
*Stockholm, May 2002*

# CONTENTS

| | | |
|---|---|---|
| Foreword | | v |
| Preface | | vii |
| 1996 | WISŁAWA SZYMBORSKA | |
| | Presentation by Birgitta Trotzig | 3 |
| | Biography of Wisława Szymborska | 7 |
| | *The Poet and the World* | 9 |
| 1997 | DARIO FO | |
| | Presentation by Sture Allén | 17 |
| | Biography of Dario Fo | 21 |
| | *Contra Jogulatores Obloquentes Against Jesters Who Defame and Insult* | 51 |
| 1998 | JOSÉ SARAMAGO | |
| | Presentation by Kjell Espmark | 89 |
| | Biography of José Saramago | 93 |
| | *How Characters Became the Masters and the Author Their Apprentice* | 97 |
| 1999 | GÜNTER GRASS | |
| | Presentation by Horace Engdahl | 111 |
| | Biography of Günter Grass | 115 |
| | *"To Be Continued..."* | 118 |
| 2000 | GAO XINGJIAN | |
| | Presentation by Göran Malmqvist | 135 |
| | Biography of Gao Xingjian | 139 |
| | *The Case for Literature* | 142 |

Literature 1996

## WISLAWA SZYMBORSKA

*"for poetry that with ironic precision allows the historical and biological context to come to light in fragments of human reality"*

# THE NOBEL PRIZE IN LITERATURE

Speech by Mrs Birgitta Trotzig, Writer, Member of the Swedish Academy.
Translation of the Swedish text.


Your Majesties, Your Royal Highness, Ladies and Gentlemen,

How are we to live after the adulteration, demise, and disintegration of the great utopias? — we ask ourselves now, looking toward the year 2000. How are we to live after the great disillusionment? With what means shall we arrive at values, by what path reach an authentic conception of life that is no longer distorted?

"Aesthetics is the mother of ethics", Brodsky says. Or: "If mankind's negative potential expresses itself in murder, its positive potential manifests itself best in art."

During the long period of the ideological recasting of human consciousness, which we have just left behind us, some of Polish postwar poetry emerged as a sign of hope, a sewage treatment plant for mutilated and contaminated language — thus for the life of the mind and the perception of life as well. In the mere existence of poetic language, in the patient word-work of distinguishing genuine from sham, false tone from true, an entire society's purification process functioned and continues to function slowly, invisibly, underground.

In Wisława Szymborska the Swedish Academy wants to honour a representative — and a representative of unusual and unyielding purity and strength — of a poetic outlook. Of poetry as a response to life, a way of life, of the word-work as thought and responsibility.

Wisława Szymborska's making of poems is the perfection of the word-object, of the exquisitely chiseled thought-image — *allegro ma non troppo*, as one of her poems is called. But a darkness that is never directly touched is perceptible, just as the movement of blood under the skin. For Szymborska, as for many other contemporary Polish poets, the starting point is the experience of a catastrophe, the ground caving in beneath her, the complete collapse of a faith. In its place human conditions break in with their inaccessibly shimmering agitation, their dailiness and pettiness, their tears and their jests, their tenderness. These conditions demand their particular language, a language that makes things relative, a language that methodically starts from scratch. The path of language is through negation — the prerequisite for being able to build anew is to build from nothing. From that point a game of role-playing begins, the wonderful dramaturgy of the world:

> Life (I say) I've no idea
> what I could compare you to.

A devotion to the mystery of surface begins here — perhaps paradoxically, perhaps the necessary life-sustaining paradox — and becomes one of the many languages of changing roles, one of the many capricious harlequin languages of transformation and identification.

In Szymborska surface is depth, the path of negation has the effect of a quiet but tremendous explosion of being. "My identifying features/are rapture and despair". The farther in one travels among the clear mirrors of her language pictures — crystalline clarity that in some way exists to lead one to a final enigma — the more one feels the world's obtrusive unambiguousness being transformed. A shimmer of wonder and of particulars hovers over the world's motionless base of rock, to whom she gives voice:

> "I don't have a door", says the stone.

I would sum up Wisława Szymborska's undertaking as a deeply transformative word-work with the state of the world. One that is best summarized in her own words in the poem *Discovery:*

> I believe in the refusal to take part.
> I believe in the ruined career.
> I believe in the wasted years of work.
> I believe in the secret taken to the grave.
> These words soar for me beyond all rules
> without seeking support from actual examples.
> My faith is strong, blind, and without foundation.

Dear Wisława Szymborska,

I am happy to convey to you, on behalf of the Swedish Academy, our warmest congratulations on the Nobel Prize in Literature for 1996 and to invite you to receive the prize from the hands of His Majesty the King.

*Translated from Swedish by Rika Lesser. Translations of poems from Wisława Szymborska: View with a Grain of Sand. Selected poems. Translated from Polish by Stanisław Barańczak and Clare Cavanagh (Harcourt Brace, 1995).*

# WISŁAWA SZYMBORSKA

Wisława Szymborska was born in Kórnik in Western Poland on 2 July 1923. Since 1931 she has been living in Kraków, where during 1945–1948 she studied Polish Literature and Sociology at the Jagiellonian University. Szymborska made her début in March 1945 with a poem "Szukam słowa" (*I am Looking for a Word*) in the daily "Dziennik Polski".

During 1953–1981 she worked as a poetry editor and columnist in the Kraków literary weekly "Życie Literackie" where the series of her essays "Lektury nadobowiązkowe" appeared (the series has been renewed lately in the addition to "Gazeta Wyborcza" — "Gazeta o Książkach"). The collection "Lektury nadobowiązkowe" was published in the form of a book four times.

Szymborska has published 18 collections of poetry: *Dlatego żyjemy* (1952), *Pytania zadawane sobie* (1954), *Wołanie do Yeti* (1957), *Sól* (1962), *Wiersze wybrane* (1964), *Poezje wybrane* (1967), *Sto pociech* (1967), *Poezje* (1970), *Wszelki wypadek* (1972), *Wybór wierszy* (1973), *Tarsjusz i inne wiersze* (1976), *Wielka liczba* (1976), *Poezje wybrane II* (1983), *Ludzie na moście* (1986). *Koniec i początek* (1993, 1996), *Widok z ziarnkiem piasku. 102 wiersze* (1996), *Życie na poczekaniu* (1997), *14 wierszy* (1998). Wisława Szymborska has also translated French poetry.

Her poems have been translated (and published in book form) in English, German, Swedish, Italian, Danish, Hebrew, Hungarian, Czech, Slovakian, Serbo-Croatian, Romanian, Bulgarian and other languages. They have also been published in many foreign anthologies of Polish poetry.

Wisława Szymborska is the Goethe Prize winner (1991) and Herder Prize winner (1995). She has a degree of Honorary Doctor of Letters of Poznań University (1995). In 1996 she received the Polish PEN Club prize.

*A selection of works by Wisława Szymborska in English*:

*People on a bridge. Poems.* Introd. and transl. by Adam Czerniawski. London, Boston: Forest Books, 1990.
*View with a grain of sand. Selected poems.* Transl. by Stanisław Barańczak and Clare Cavanagh. New York: Harcourt Brace and Co., 1995.
*Nothing twice. Selected poems.* Selected and transl. by Stanisław Barańczak and Clare Cavanagh. Kraków: Wydawn. Literackie, 1997.
*Poems, new and collected, 1957–1997.* Transl. by Stanisław Barańczak and Clare Cavanagh. New York: Harcourt Brace, 1998.
*Miracle fair. Selected poems.* Transl. by Joanna Trzeciak. New York: Norton, 2001.
*Nonrequired reading. Prose pieces.* Transl. by Clare Cavanagh. New York: Harcourt, Inc., 2002.

# THE POET AND THE WORLD

Nobel Lecture, December 7, 1996
by
WISŁAWA SZYMBORSKA
Kraków, Poland


They say the first sentence in any speech is always the hardest. Well, that one's behind me, anyway. But I have a feeling that the sentences to come — the third, the sixth, the tenth, and so on, up to the final line — will be just as hard, since I'm supposed to talk about poetry. I've said very little on the subject, next to nothing, in fact. And whenever I have said anything, I've always had the sneaking suspicion that I'm not very good at it. This is why my lecture will be rather short. All imperfection is easier to tolerate if served up in small doses.

Contemporary poets are skeptical and suspicious even, or perhaps especially, about themselves. They publicly confess to being poets only reluctantly, as if they were a little ashamed of it. But in our clamorous times it's much easier to acknowledge your faults, at least if they're attractively packaged, than to recognize your own merits, since these are hidden deeper and you never quite believe in them yourself ... When filling in questionnaires or chatting with strangers, that is, when they can't avoid revealing their profession, poets prefer to use the general term "writer" or replace "poet" with the name of whatever job they do in addition to writing. Bureaucrats and bus passengers respond with a touch of incredulity and alarm when they find out that they're dealing with a poet. I suppose philosophers may meet with a similar reaction. Still, they're in a better position, since as often as not they can embellish their calling with some kind of scholarly title. Professor of philosophy — now that sounds much more respectable.

But there are no professors of poetry. This would mean, after all, that poetry is an occupation requiring specialized study, regular examinations, theoretical articles with bibliographies and footnotes attached, and finally, ceremoniously conferred diplomas. And this would mean, in turn, that it's not enough to cover pages with even the most exquisite poems in order to become a poet. The crucial element is some slip of paper bearing an official stamp. Let us recall that the pride of Russian poetry, the future Nobel Laureate Joseph Brodsky, was once sentenced to internal exile precisely on such grounds. They called him "a parasite," because he lacked official certification granting him the right to be a poet...

Several years ago, I had the honor and pleasure of meeting Brodsky in person. And I noticed that, of all the poets I've known, he was the only one who enjoyed calling himself a poet. He pronounced the word without inhibitions.

Just the opposite — he spoke it with defiant freedom. It seems to me that this must have been because he recalled the brutal humiliations he had experienced in his youth.

In more fortunate countries, where human dignity isn't assaulted so readily, poets yearn, of course, to be published, read, and understood, but they do little, if anything, to set themselves above the common herd and the daily grind. And yet it wasn't so long ago, in this century's first decades, that poets strove to shock us with their extravagant dress and eccentric behavior. But all this was merely for the sake of public display. The moment always came when poets had to close the doors behind them, strip off their mantles, fripperies, and other poetic paraphernalia, and confront — silently, patiently awaiting their own selves — the still white sheet of paper. For this is finally what really counts.

It's not accidental that film biographies of great scientists and artists are produced in droves. The more ambitious directors seek to reproduce convincingly the creative process that led to important scientific discoveries or the emergence of a masterpiece. And one can depict certain kinds of scientific labor with some success. Laboratories, sundry instruments, elaborate machinery brought to life: such scenes may hold the audience's interest for a while. And those moments of uncertainty — will the experiment, conducted for the thousandth time with some tiny modification, finally yield the desired result? — can be quite dramatic. Films about painters can be spectacular, as they go about recreating every stage of a famous painting's evolution, from the first penciled line to the final brush stroke. Music swells in films about composers: the first bars of the melody that rings in the musician's ears finally emerge as a mature work in symphonic form. Of course this is all quite naive and doesn't explain the strange mental state popularly known as inspiration, but at least there's something to look at and listen to.

But poets are the worst. Their work is hopelessly unphotogenic. Someone sits at a table or lies on a sofa while staring motionless at a wall or ceiling. Once in a while this person writes down seven lines only to cross out one of them fifteen minutes later, and then another hour passes, during which nothing happens ... Who could stand to watch this kind of thing?

I've mentioned inspiration. Contemporary poets answer evasively when asked what it is, and if it actually exists. It's not that they've never known the blessing of this inner impulse. It's just not easy to explain something to someone else that you don't understand yourself.

When I'm asked about this on occasion, I hedge the question too. But my answer is this: inspiration is not the exclusive privilege of poets or artists generally. There is, has been, and will always be a certain group of people whom inspiration visits. It's made up of all those who've consciously chosen their calling and do their job with love and imagination. It may include doctors, teachers, gardeners — and I could list a hundred more professions. Their work becomes one continuous adventure as long as they manage to keep discovering new challenges in it. Difficulties and setbacks never quell their curiosity. A swarm of new questions emerges from every problem they solve. Whatever inspiration is, it's born from a continuous "I don't know."

There aren't many such people. Most of the earth's inhabitants work to get by. They work because they have to. They didn't pick this or that kind of job out of passion; the circumstances of their lives did the choosing for them. Loveless work, boring work, work valued only because others haven't got even that much, however loveless and boring — this is one of the harshest human miseries. And there's no sign that coming centuries will produce any changes for the better as far as this goes.

And so, though I may deny poets their monopoly on inspiration, I still place them in a select group of Fortune's darlings.

At this point, though, certain doubts may arise in my audience. All sorts of torturers, dictators, fanatics, and demagogues struggling for power by way of a few loudly shouted slogans also enjoy their jobs, and they too perform their duties with inventive fervor. Well, yes, but they "know." They know, and whatever they know is enough for them once and for all. They don't want to find out about anything else, since that might diminish their arguments' force.

And any knowledge that doesn't lead to new questions quickly dies out: it fails to maintain the temperature required for sustaining life. In the most extreme cases, cases well known from ancient and modern history, it even poses a lethal threat to society.

This is why I value that little phrase "I don't know" so highly. It's small, but it flies on mighty wings. It expands our lives to include the spaces within us as well as those outer expanses in which our tiny Earth hangs suspended. If Isaac Newton had never said to himself "I don't know," the apples in his little orchard might have dropped to the ground like hailstones and at best he would have stooped to pick them up and gobble them with gusto. Had my compatriot Marie Skłodowska-Curie never said to herself "I don't know," she probably would have wound up teaching chemistry at some private high school for young ladies from good families, and would have ended her days performing this otherwise perfectly respectable job. But she kept on saying "I don't know," and these words led her, not just once but twice, to Stockholm, where restless, questing spirits are occasionally rewarded with the Nobel Prize.

Poets, if they're genuine, must also keep repeating "I don't know." Each poem marks an effort to answer this statement, but as soon as the final period hits the page, the poet begins to hesitate, starts to realize that this particular answer was pure makeshift that's absolutely inadequate to boot. So the poets keep on trying, and sooner or later the consecutive results of their self-dissatisfaction are clipped together with a giant paperclip by literary historians and called their "oeuvre"...

I sometimes dream of situations that can't possibly come true. I audaciously imagine, for example, that I get a chance to chat with the Ecclesiastes, the author of that moving lament on the vanity of all human endeavors. I would bow very deeply before him, because he is, after all, one of the greatest poets, for me at least. That done, I would grab his hand. "'There's nothing new under the sun': that's what you wrote, Ecclesiastes. But you yourself were born new under the sun. And the poem you created is also new under the sun, since no one wrote it down before you. And all your readers are also new under the sun, since those who lived before you couldn't read your poem. And that cypress that you're sitting under hasn't been growing since the dawn of time. It came into being by way of another cypress similar to yours, but not exactly the same. And Ecclesiastes, I'd also like to ask you what new thing under the sun you're planning to work on now? A further supplement to the thoughts you've already expressed? Or maybe you're tempted to contradict some of them now? In your earlier work you mentioned joy — so what if it's fleeting? So maybe your new-under-the-sun poem will be about joy? Have you taken notes yet, do you have drafts? I doubt you'll say, 'I've written everything down, I've got nothing left to add. There's no poet in the world who can say this, least of all a great poet like yourself."

The world — whatever we might think when terrified by its vastness and our own impotence, or embittered by its indifference to individual suffering, of people, animals, and perhaps even plants, for why are we so sure that plants feel no pain; whatever we might think of its expanses pierced by the rays of stars surrounded by planets we've just begun to discover, planets already dead? still dead? we just don't know; whatever we might think of this measureless theater to which we've got reserved tickets, but tickets whose lifespan is laughably short, bounded as it is by two arbitrary dates; whatever else we might think of this world — it is astonishing.

But "astonishing" is an epithet concealing a logical trap. We're astonished, after all, by things that deviate from some well-known and universally acknowledged norm, from an obviousness we've grown accustomed to, Now the point is, there is no such obvious world. Our astonishment exists per se and isn't based on comparison with something else.

Granted, in daily speech, where we don't stop to consider every word, we all use phrases like "the ordinary world," "ordinary life," "the ordinary course of events" ... But in the language of poetry, where every word is weighed, nothing is usual or normal. Not a single stone and not a single cloud above it. Not a single day and not a single night after it. And above all, not a single existence, not anyone's existence in this world.

It looks like poets will always have their work cut out for them.

*Translated from Polish by Stanisław Barańczak and Clare Cavanagh*

Literature 1997

# DARIO FO

*"who emulates the jesters of the Middle Ages in scourging authority and upholding the dignity of the down-trodden"*

# THE NOBEL PRIZE IN LITERATURE

Speech by Professor Sture Allén of the Swedish Academy.
Translation of the Swedish text.

Your Majesties, Your Royal Highnesses, Ladies and Gentlemen,

To be a jester is, and always has been, a serious matter. Swedish mediaeval laws stipulated that it cost a man smaller fines to lay violent hands on some-body from a neighbouring county than on a man from his own part of the country; but to assault a jester, on the other hand, cost him nothing at all. If a jester is beaten up, says the thirteenth-century law concerning such people, it shall not be counted an offence. If a jester comes to bodily harm, he shall have and suffer what was given him — infamy and injury. "Let him never appeal for more justice than a thral woman lashed on her bare back."

One of Dario Fo's sources of inspiration is exactly these mediaeval jesters, unprotected by any law. According to Fo satire is what makes the most forceful impact on man. Mixing laughter and seriousness is his way of telling the truth about abuses and unrighteousness. For Alfred Nobel literary achievements were important means for fulfilling the fundamental aim of the awards, namely to confer benefit on mankind. The maintenance of human dignity is unquestionably an essential aspect of this.

Fo often refers explicitly to the mediaeval joculatores and their comedy and mysteries. In fact, a central work in his oeuvre, "Mistero buffo" — "The Comic Mysteries", is based on old material culled from many different quarters. In the scene called "The Birth of the Jester" the crucial moment occurs when a landlord avid for more land violates the wife of the man who is breaking untilled ground. "The Marriage at Cana" is seen from the point of view of the intoxicated wine-drinker. In "The Resurrection of Lazarus" the provocative question is whether Jesus will succeed.

There are several other sources. Furthest away in time we seem to glimpse Plautus and Terence in Rome, who were of renewed interest in fifteenth century Italy. The commedia dell'arte, a creation of the sixteenth century, is of importance with its set-character parts and its oral tradition. It is also possible to catch a sly glance from Bottom the weaver and Sir Andrew Aguecheek. Impulses from our own days come from Mayakovsky's epic-satirical poetry and from Brecht's didactic theatre. Incidentally, it was from Mayakovsky that Fo borrowed the title "Mistero Buffo".

Another major achievement in Fo's large production is "Accidental Death of an Anarchist". The play is about the cross-examining following on the supposed accident. By and by the questioning is taken over, through a brilliantly carried out shift, by a Hamlet-like figure — il Matto — who has the kind of madness that exposes official falsehoods. All in all there are many topical allusions in Fo's plays, but the texts transcend everyday situations and are given a far wider range of application.

One cannot hold it against Fo that he is a first-rate actor. The decisive thing is that he has written plays which arouse the enthusiasm of actors and which captivate his audiences. The texts are chiselled in an interplay with the spectators and have often been given their final shape over a long time. Rapidly changing situations give impetus to the plays and shape the characters. The rhythm of the actors' lines, the witty wording and the aptitude for improvisation combine with strong intensity and artistic energy in the profoundly meaningful, steady flow of his flashes of wit. The printed texts can also give you this feeling if you give free range to your imagination. Fo's work brings to the fore the multifarious abundance of the literary field.

His independence and perspicacity have made him run great risks and right enough he has been made to experience the consequences both at home and abroad. When on one occasion he and his wife, Franca Rame, had been stopped from making an agreed-on appearance abroad, their friends and colleagues arranged a representation which they called "An Evening without Dario Fo and Franca Rame".

Looking backwards in time from Dario Fo, the ninety-fourth laureate for literature, to earlier writers given the award, it is tempting to arrest oneself at George Bernard Shaw, winner of the Prize seventy years ago. On that occasion the Swedish Academy emphasised the laureate's idealism, humanity, and stimulating satire. The two writers are no doubt different from each other, but the same evaluative words can be applied to Dario Fo.

Dear Mr. Fo,

The word dignity plays an important part in your oeuvre and is at the centre of the piece called "The Birth of the Jester". The dignity bestowed on you today may have other attributes, but it has the same core. On behalf of the Swedish Academy I congratulate you warmly on the work which has resulted in the Nobel Prize in Literature 1997 and I ask you to step forward to receive the prize from the hands of His Majesty the King.

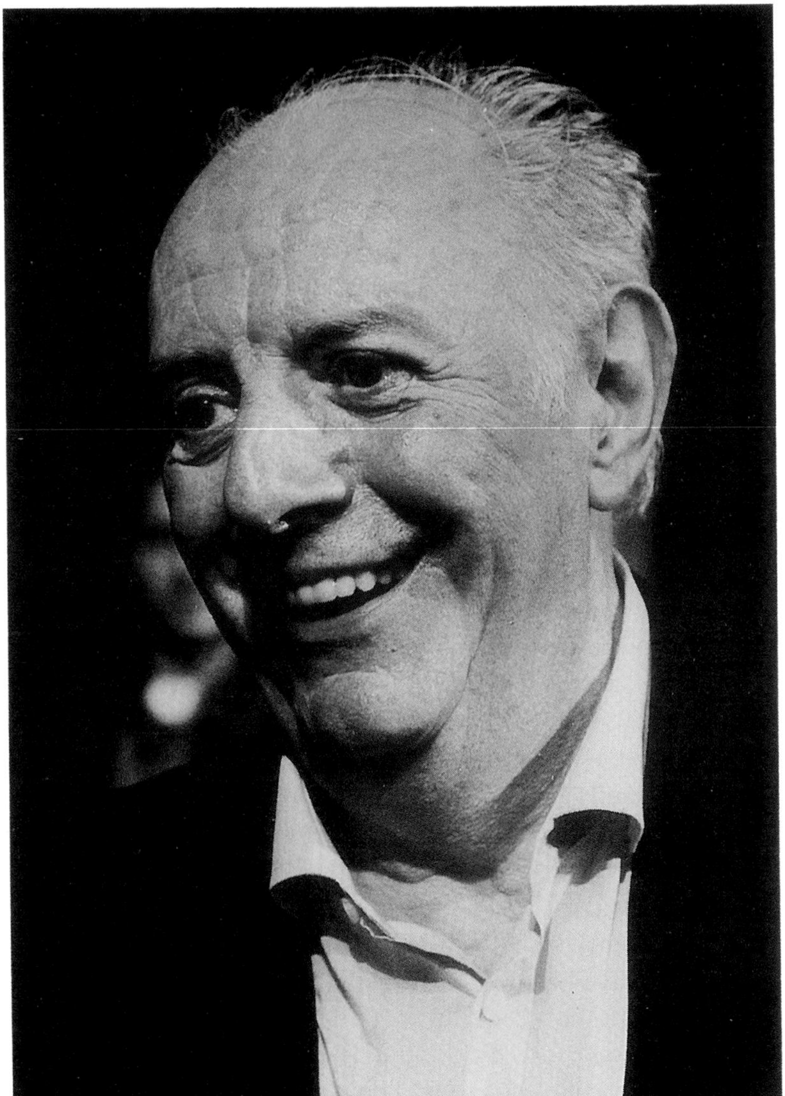

Dario Fo

# DARIO FO

In addition to playwright, Dario Fo is also director, stage and costume designer, and on occasion he even composes the music for his plays.

Franca Rame, in addition to being his leading actress, has assisted in and contributed to the writing of many of the plays they have produced in their 45 years of theatre together. She has also assumed the administrative and organizational responsibility for the Fo–Rame Company.

FRANCA RAME

Franca Rame was born in Parabiago, a small town in the Province of Milan. That she happened to be born there was pure chance: her family was performing in the town at the time. Her father Domenico, her mother Emilia and her brother, along with aunts, uncles, cousins and other actors and actresses hired on contract, were all part of a travelling theatre troupe touring the towns and villages of Lombardy and Piedmont.

The Rame family's ties to the theatre are very old. Since the late 17th century, they have been actors, and puppet masters, as the occasion required.

With the arrival of the cinema they shifted from puppet theatre to real theatre, enriched with all the "special effects" of the puppet theatre. They travelled from town to town, and were well received wherever they went.

Even today, her personal success in theatre and television notwithstanding, people in these towns still often refer to Franca as "the daughter of Domenico Rame". In the best tradition of the Commedia dell'Arte, the family improvised its performances, drawing on a rich repertoire of tragic and comical situations and dialogues.

They often opened in a new town — following a poll among the towns-people — with an enactment of the life of the local patron saint.

The family's repertoire ranged from the biblical texts over Shakespeare to Chekhov and Pirandello, from Niccodemi to the great 19th century historical novels — especially those with a socialist or anticlerical bent. Often their performances included enactments of the lives of men such as Giordano Bruno, Arnaldo da Brescia and Galileo Galilei.

Domenico Rame was the troupe's poet; a devout socialist, he often saw to it that the revenue from a performance was given in support of striking workers or used to build child-care facilities, or in other ways spent to improve the lives of the common people. The minutely documented records of this activity, which remains in the Rame–Fo archives, was probably maintained by Franca's mother Emilia Baldini, a school teacher and daughter of a municipal engineer in Bobbio.

As a young school teacher, Emilia fell in love with Domenico — twenty years her senior — who was passing through Bobbio with his marionettes and puppets. She married him, against the strong wishes of her family, and together they continued to tour all of Lombardy. Emilia soon learned the trades of acting and costume designer. It was she who taught their four children to act and to move on the stage. She was an outstanding woman, meticulous in all her work and an excellent organizer. In the end it was she who carried the troupe on her shoulders.

It was in this environment that Franca earned her apprenticeship. She has always felt at home on the stage because — as she says — "I was born there: I was only eight days old when I made my debut in my mother's arms [she played the new-born son of Geneviève of Brabant] ... I didn't say much that evening!".

Some years later, in the 1950–51 theatre seasson, Franca — following the lead of her sister Pia — left the family and joined the company of Tino Scotti for a part in Marcello Marchesi's "Ghe pensi mi" at the Teatro Olimpia in Milan.

## DARIO FO

Dario Fo was born on 26 March 1926 in San Giano, a small town on Lago Maggiore in the province of Varese. His family consisted of: his father Felice, socialist, station master and actor in an amateur theatre company; his mother Pina Rota, a woman of great imagination and talent (in the 1970s her auto-biographical account

"Il paese delle rane", telling the history of her home town, was published by Einaudi); his brother Fulvio and his sister Bianca; and his maternal grandfather, who had a farm in Lomellina, where young Dario spent his childhood vacations.

During Dario's visits, his grandfather would travel around the countryside selling his produce from a big, horse-drawn wagon. To attract customers he would tell the most amazing stories, and in these stories he would insert news and anecdotes about local events. His satirical and timely chronicles earned him the nickname *Bristìn* (pepper seed). It was from his grandfather, sitting beside him on the big wagon, that Dario began to learn the rudiments of narrative rhythm.

Dario spent his childhood moving from one town to another, as his father's postings were changed at the whim of the railway authorities. But even though the geography remained in a flux, the cultural setting was always the same. As the boy grew, he became schooled in the local narrative tradition. With growing passion, he would sit in the taverns or the *piazze* and listen tirelessly to the master glass-blowers and fishermen, who — in the oral tradition of the *fabulatore* — would swap tall tales, steeped in pungent political satire.

In 1940 he moved to Milan (commuting from Luino) to study at the Brera Art Academy. After the war, he begins to study architecture at the Polytechnic, but interrupts his studies with only a few exams left to complete his degree.

Towards the end of the war, Dario is conscripted into the army of the Salò republic. He manages to escape, and spends the last months of the war hidden in an attic store room. His parents are active in the resistance, his father organizing the smuggling of Jewish scientists and escaped British prisoners of war into Switzerland by train; his mother caring for wounded partisans.

At the end of the war, Dario returns to his studies at the Academy of Brera in Milan while attending courses in architecture at the Polytechnic, commuting each day from his home on Lago Maggiore.

1945–41 he turns his attention to stage design and theatre décor. He begins to improvise monologues.

He moves with his family to Milan. Mamma Fo, in order to help her husband put the three children through college, does her best as a shirt-maker.

For the younger Fos, this is a period of ravenous reading. Gramsci and Marx are devoured along with American novelists and the first translations of Brecht, Mayakovsky and Lorca.

In the immediate postwar years, Italian theatre undergoes a veritable revolution, pushed along mainly by the new phenomenon of *piccoli teatri* ["small theatres"] that play a key role in developing the idea of a "popular stage".

Fo is captured by this effervescent movement and proves to be an insatiable theatregoer — even though he usually can't afford to buy a seat and has to stand through the performances. Mamma Fo keeps an open mind and an open house for her children's new acquaintances, among them Emilio Tadini, Alik Cavalieri, Piccoli, Vittorini, Morlotti, Treccani, Crepax, some of them already famous.

During his architecture studies, while working as decorator and assistant architect, Dario begins to entertain his friends with tales as tall as those he heard in the lakeside taverns of his childhood.

In the summer of 1950, Dario seeks out Franco Parenti who is enthralled by the young man's comical rendering of the parable of Cain and Abel, a satire in which Cain, *poer nano* ["poor little thing"], a miserable fool, is anything but evil. It's just that every time he tries, *poer nano*, to mimic the splendid, blond and blue-eyed Abel, he gets into trouble. After suffering one disaster after another, he finally goes crazy and kills the splendid Abel. Franco Parenti enthusiastically invites Fo to join his theatre company.

Dario starts performing in Parenti's summer variety show. This is when he has his first "encounter" with Franca Rame – not in person, mind, but in the form of a photograph he sees at the home of some friends. He is thunder-struck!

For a while he continues to work as assistant architect. But he soon decides to abandon his work and studies, disgusted by the corruption already rampant in the building sector.

# CHRONOLOGY

*The 1951–52 theatre season* — Franca Rame and Dario Fo meet by chance: they are both engaged in a production of **"Sette giorni a Milano"** by Spiller and Carosso, staged by the Nava-Parenti company at the Odeon Theatre in Milan.
Dario's courting technique is drastic: he pretends not to see Franca. After a couple of weeks of this, she grabs him backstage, pushes him up against a wall and gives him a passionate kiss. They are engaged.

1951 — Fo's performance is a minor success, and he is invited to participate in RAI's (the Italian national radio's) show **"Cocoricò"**, where he earns a certain notoriety with his "poer nano" monologues, transmitted in 18 episodes. His innovative use of language subverts the rhetoric of "official" narrative. It is the first experiment with a narrative technique that combines re-examinations of history with excursions into popular lore, a technique he is later to develop further with **"Mistero boffo"**. Created in this period are his grotesque renditions of the stories of Cain and Abel, Samson and Delilah, Abraham and Isaac, Romeo and Juliet, Moses, Othello, Rigoletto, Hamlet, Julius Caesar, King David, Nero and others.
The series is interrupted after the eighteenth show, as the producers — who are slow to catch on to the social and political satire that permeates the monologues — at last see fit to censure them.

1951–52 — Dario makes his debut with a series of monologues entitled **"Poer Nano"** ("poor little thing", an affectionate expression in the Lombard dialect) in the revue **"Sette giorni a Milano"**, where he meets Franca Rame. Fo's monologues are a success, leading to an own show on Italian national radio. He becomes a celebrity.

1952 — **"Papaveri e papere"**, a film by Marcello Marchesi, with Franca Rame and Walter Chiari. Franca has roles in some ten-odd other commercial films.

| | |
|---|---|
| 1952–53 | Dario Fo is on stage with the satirical performance **"Cocoricò"**, with Giustino Durano, Viky Enderson and others.<br>Franca Rame is engaged by Remigio Paone to play in a big revue company, Billi and Riva in **"I fanatici"** by Marchesi and Mertz, music by Kramer. Teatro Nuovo, Milan. |
| 1953–54 | For a performance at the Piccolo Teatro in Milan, Fo writes, together with Franco Parenti and Giustino Durano, directs (in collaboration with Lecoq) and plays **"Il dito nell'occhio"**. (He is also responsible for stage design and costumes.) Franca Rame also participates in the production, which is the first really satirical post-war revue. The show sparks both approval and controversy. The company has difficulty in finding theatres to stage the play. Drastic efforts of censorship by the government as well as the Church: signs on church doors exhort parishioners not to see the play. This becomes a praxis that will hound the Fo–Rame theatre company for many years. |
| 24 June | Franca and Dario are married in Milan's Saint Ambrose Basilica. From this moment on, Franca is Fo's main collaborator behind the desk as well as on the stage. |
| 1954–55 | Together with Parenti and Durano, Fo writes and at the Piccolo Teatro in Milan, directs and plays **"I sani da legare"**. Also this play is subject to the same type of censorship as is described above. These two plays are the first real satirical postwar revues, and both enjoy great success with the public. |
| 1955 | Attracted by the possibility to work in the cinema, the couple moves to Rome. Dario works as screenwriter (gag-man) with Age, Scarpelli, Scola and Pinelli, and for Ponti and De Laurentiis as well as for other productions. |
| 31 March | Their son Jacopo is born.<br>Franca with Memo Benassi in **"King Lear"** at the Teatro Stabile of Bolzano. |
| 1956 | Fo writes the script for and plays against Franca Rame in the film **"Lo svitato"**, directed by Carlo Lizzani. |

| | |
|---|---|
| 1956–57 | Fo collaborates in various film script projects and plays against Franca in several films. |
| 1957 | Franca Rame in **"Non andartene in giro tntta nuda"** ["Mais n'te promène donc pas tout nue!"] by G. Feydeau at the Arlecchino Theatre in Rome. |
| 1957–58 | The "Fo–Rame Company" is established. Franca and Dario return to Milan to establish their own theatre company, with Dario as playwright, actor, director, stage- and costume-designer. Franca is Dario's main text collaborator and leading actress. She also assumes responsibility for the company's administration.
The Fo–Rame company makes its debut at Milan's Piccolo Teatro. The company then leaves for a first long, annual tour (there were to be many, lasting up to 10 months and bringing the company to every part of Italy) with a performance entitled "**Ladri, manichini e donne nude**" and comprising four one-act farces: **"l'uomo nudo, l'uomo in frack"** ["**One Was Nude and One Wore Tails**"], **"Non tntti i ladri vengono per nuocere"** ["**The Virtnous Burglar**"], **"Gli imbianchini non hanno ricordi"** and **"I cadaveri si spediscono e le donne si spogliano"**. The four farces make the most of an endless series of misunderstandings, mistaken identities, people running up and down stairs, gags and slapstick. |
| 1958–59 | **"Comica finale"** is another collection of four one-act plays: **"Quando sarai povero sarai re"**, **"La Marcolfa"**, **"Un morto da vendere"** and **"I tre bravi"**. These are short, comical stories structured much like the ones Franca's family played at the end of their performances ("comic closures"). From the Teatro Stabile, Dario Fo and Franca Rame buy scenery, props and costumes, and set out on tour with their company. They also revive "Ladri, manichini e donne nude". |

## THE FO–RAME COMPANY HAS ITS FIRST OPENING AT A MAJOR, DOWNTOWN THEATRE IN MILAN

1959–60     With **"Gli arcangeli non giocano a flipper"** [**"Archangels Don't Play Pinball"**], at Milan's Odeon Theatre, The Fo–Rame Company finally earns national recognition. The play becomes the greatest box-office hit in Italian theatre.

1960     Fo writes **"La storia vera di Piero d'Angera, che alla crociata non c'era"**, produced by other companies with great success.

1960–61     Teatro Odeon, Milan: **"Aveva due pistole con gli occhi bianchi e neri"**.

1961     First performance abroad with his play: **"Ladri, manichini e donne nude"**, first at Stockholm's Arena Theatre, then with a production in Poland.

1961–62     Teatro Odeon, Milan: **"Chi ruba un piede è fortunato in amore"**.

1962     In the spring, RAI (Italian national television) broadcasts on its second channel the televised variety show **"Chi l'ha visto?"** with Fo–Rame and others.

Together with Franca Rame, Dario Fo is invited to write, direct and present **"Canzonissima"**, a highly popular IV show built around the national lottery, with a different host each year. Fo's and Rame's sketches become an issue for the entire nation, provoking wild controversy. For the first time, television is used to portray the lives and difficulties of common people: the work-related illness of a signal woman, bricklayers that fall to their death from the scaffolding, etc.

The show is very successful; during broadcasts even taxi drivers stop working, and bars with televisions are smack full of people. RAI's management starts to get nervous. Cuts are demanded in texts that have already been approved. All hell breaks loose over a sketch with a Mafia theme that tells the story of a murdered journalist. Malagodi, a senator from Italy's Liberal Party, reports the sketch to the Italian Parliament's oversight committee for television, on the grounds that "the honour of the Sicilian people is insulted by the claim that there exists a criminal organization called the Mafia". (In 1985, Prime Minister Andreotti appoints Malagodi senator-for-life for his political services.) Fo and Rame also receive death threats, written with blood and delivered with the typical miniature, wooden coffin. The Fo family (including Franca's and Dario's seven-year-old son) is placed under police protection.

A fight begins with RAI about censorship. Just a few hours before the scheduled broadcast of the eighth programme in the series, RAI's management declares that further cuts must be made. Dario and Franca refuse and threaten to leave the programme. As **"Canzonissima"** is about to be aired it is still unclear what is going to happen. At the last minute RAI confirms the cuts. Dario and Franca walk off the show as a sign of protest.

The support they receive for their act is overwhelming, including thousands of letters and telegrams. RAI is unable to find substitutes for Fo and Rame, as all who are asked to replace them follow the instructions of SAI (the Italian actors' union) to turn down the offer.

Fo and Rame face five law suits as a consequence and are ordered to pay several billion lire in damages. For 15 years they are banned by RAI from participating in either programmes or commercials on national radio or television (at that time, both radio and television were state monopolies).

1963–64  Opening at Milan's Odeon Theatre of **"Isabella, tre caravelle e un cacciaballe"**, which tells the story of the "discovery" of America on the basis of a thorough historical investigation of the life of Christopher Columbus, the court of Isabella of Castille and the "ethnic cleansing" of Spain's Arabs and Jews. The play marks the beginning of a major effort to trace the history and "dogmas" of the dominant culture. The play, blatantly exposing the mystifications of "school-book" history and of militarist and patriotic rhetoric, comes under violent attack by right-wing groups. On one occasion, Fo and Rame are assaulted as they leave the Valle Theatre in Rome. Only through the presence of groups of militant workers from the Italian Communist Party (PCI) can the performances continue.

1964–65 **"Settimo: ruba un po' meno"** opens at the Odeon in Milan. The play is dedicated to Franca Rame, who in the leading comic role portrays a rather odd grave digger whose highest ambition is to become a prostitute. With its minutely detailed description of the corruption rampant in Italy, it anticipates by some thirty years the revolution brought about by the **"Mani Pulite"** ("Clean hands") movement.

1965–66 Milan's Odeon Theatre: **"La colpa è sempre del diavolo"**.

1966–67 Two productions: **"Gli amici della battoniera"**, translated from French and adapted by Fo; and **"Ci ragiono e canto"**, in collaboration with Nuovo Canzoniere Italiano, a performance built on traditional folk songs, compiled by Gianni Bosio and elaborated by Fo.

1967 Following the Soviet invasion of Czechoslovakia, Dario Fo withdraws his permission for his plays to be staged in Czech theatres. He later refuses to authorize cuts, proposed by Soviet censors, in a play scheduled to open at a Soviet theatre. After these incidents, production of his work all but ceases throughout the Soviet block.

1967–68 Teatro Manzoni in Milan: **"La signora è da buttare"**.

1968–69 Stimulated by the political events of those years, Dario and Franca disband their company and establish the Associazione Nuova Scena, composed of more than thirty young technicians, actors and actresses. It is an independent theatre collective, organized in three groups that tour Italy with productions staged mainly before working class audiences and at venues other than those offered by the official theatre circuit, such as *case del popolo* (workers' community halls), sport arenas, cinemas, boccia courts, town squares, etc. To allow mobility and use of available space, foldable stages are built on Dario's design. Nuova Scena's first production opens at the *Casa del popolo* in Cesena (Romagna) with a performance of "**Grande pantomima per pupazzi piccoli, grandi e medi**". The production is also staged at Milan's Union Hall and is played on tour. Back in Milan, Nuova Scena — encountering difficulties in finding a fixed venue — rents an old, abandoned factory which it transforms into a theatrical centre. The centre becomes the home stage of a new company, *Il Capannone di Via Colletta*, supported by the theatre collective and by a large group of members: workers and students who contribute with their creativity and practical skills.

**1969–70** At Genua's Union Hall and in various localities, Franca Rame is on stage with two new comic productions by Fo: "**L'operaio conosce 300 parole, il padrone 1000, per questo lui è il padrone**" and a double feature consisting of two one-act farces: "**Legami pure, tanto spacco tutto lo stesso**" and "**Il funerale del padrone**". Because of the plays' expressed critique of Stalinism and of the social-democratic position of the Italian Communist Party, the tour is heavily sabotaged by the Party leadership. Some ten-odd performances are cancelled. The situation is very tense, Franca's planned opening at Milan's Union Hall is cancelled. Instead she is invited to play at the "**Circus Medini**", a real circus with horses, tigers, lions and elephants, luckily all kept in cages around the tent. After some initial difficulties, the production can continue — thanks to support organized among the Party rank and file and among the extraparliamentary left — to enjoy great public success. Franca sends her Party card back to PCI Secretary Enrico Berlinguer (Dario has never been a member).

Dario stages "**Mistero buffo**" ["**Mistero Buffo**"]. The performance takes the form of a lesson in the history of literature that departs from a questioning of school dogma, in particular the text-book interpretation of the earliest known text in Italian (**"Rosa fresca e aulentissima"**), in which the text's blatant — and scurrilous — allusion to the feminine genitalia is altogether censored. The actor reconstructs the language of the medieval jesters, reciting their monologues in such a way as to make them accessible to a wide audience today. The play is a terrific success; it even becomes necessary to stage it at sport arenas that can hold thousands. It is the play that more than any other establishes Fo's fame worldwide. More than 5000 performances.

Due to political differences, Dario Fo and Franca Rame leave "Nuova Scena". The "Collettivo Teatrale La Comune" sees the light of day, directed by Dario Fo and Franca Rame.

1970–71   1970 Arturo Corso begins as assistant director to Fo. La Comune produces (at the *Capannone di via Colletta*): **"Vorrei morire anche stasera se dovessi sapere che non è servito niente"**, a play about the Italian and Palestinian resistance.

Following the terrorist attack on the Banca Nazionale dell'Agricoltura in Milan, Dario writes and produces one of his most famous pieces: **"Morte accidentale di un anarchico"** [**"Accidental Death of an Anarchist"**], about the *strage di Stato* [a massacre thought to be organized by organs of the state].

Franca Rame on stage in **"Tutti uniti, tutti inseme! Ma, scusa, quello non è il padrone?!"**, a play about the birth of the Italian Communist Party in 1921.

1971   **"Fedayin"**, a piece by Fo, with Franca on stage with 10 authentic Palestinian freedom fighters to gather funds and medicine for the Palestinian resistance. Franca went to fetch the fedayeen herself in the training camps in Lebanon, with the help of the Popular Democratic Front.

1971–72   **"Ordine per Dio.ooo.ooo.ooo"** with Franca Rame and other actors, while Dario tours Italy with **"Mistero buffo numero 2"**. Due to the economic crisis, many factories are closed. To defend their jobs, workers go on strike and occupy the factories. In support of this struggle, from 1971 to 1985 the La Comune collective stages hundreds of performances, donating the revenues to the workers.

La Comune is forced to leave the *Capannone di via Colletta*. The contract has expired and the owner refuses to renew it.

1973–74  Dario, Franca and their colleagues are not deterred. They rent the Rossini Cinema on the outskirts of Milan, where they stage **"Pum pum, chi è? La Polizia!"** [**"Bang bang, who's there? Police!"**] (still addressing the *strage di Stato*) with Dario Fo and other actors.

The theatre collective is subjected to various acts of repression by the police as well as to efforts at censorship.

8 March  A group of fascists kidnaps, tortures and rapes Franca Rame.

Through this beastly act, they seek to punish Franca and Dario for their political activism, in particular Franca's work in the prisons since 1970. Outcries of indignation and support throughout Italy.

May  Following a two-month break, Franca returns to the stage with a performance entitled **"Basta con i fascisti"**, a slide presentation with monologues by Fo–Rame and Lanfranco Binni. The performance is dedicated to young people and addresses the cultural and political presence of fascism within the Italian state, retelling the birth, history and violence of fascism (opening: Milan's *Casa del popolo* and tour).

Paris: **"Mistero buffo"** with Théâtre National Populaire at Salle Gemier–Trocadero.

**"Ci ragiono e canto N.3"** written by Fo for the Sicilian street singer Ciccio Busacca.

Having searched in vain for a permanent stage, La Comune occupies an abandoned, dilapidated building in central Milan, the *Palazzina Liberty*, formerly an indoor vegetable market. Within a year they have 80 000 season-ticket holders in Milan alone.

| | |
|---|---|
| September | A few days after the death of Allende, La Comune opens its new home stage — repaired and put in order with the help of neighbours and workers from various Milan factories — with **"Guerra di popolo in Cile"**. The revenues go to the Chilean resistance. During a guest performance in Sassari, Fo is arrested for having blocked access to the theatre for policemen seeking to stop the performance. |
| 1974–75 | *Palazzina Liberty*: **"Non si paga, non si paga!"** [**"Can't pay? Won't pay!"**]. In the course of the season, Fo and Rame organize performances, demonstrations and concerts in support of the campaign for a referendum on divorce and as manifestations of solidarity with workers occupying factories and in other ways taking part in the political struggle. Many immigrants have in the *Palazzina Liberty* found a place to meet to discuss their common concerns and to celebrate their faiths. |
| June 1975 | **"Fanfani rapito"**: Fo writes this piece in four days in support of the campaign for a referendum for the legalization of abortion. The performances of **"Non si paga, non si paga!"** are interrupted and the new play is staged within eight days! |
| 1975 | The La Comune collective visits the People's Republic of China for one month. A group of Swedish intellectuals nominate Fo as candidate for the Nobel Prize in literature. |
| 1975–76 | **"La marijuana della mamma é la più bella"**, a play about the drug fad making headway also in Italy. |
| 1976–77 | On the invitation of Massimo Fichera, Director of RAI 2, Dario and Franca return to television after 15 years. The series **"Il teatro di Dario Fo"** includes **"Mistero buffo"**, **"Settimo: ruba on po' meno!"**, **"Ci ragiono e canto"**, **"Isabella, tre caravelle e un cacciaballe"**, **"La signora è da buttare"** and **"Parliamo di donne"**, for a total television time of 21 hours. The political right and the Church complain ... and attack the programme at every opportunity! Franca Rame receives the IDI Prize as best television actress for her performance in **"Parliamo di donne"**. |

1977–78 During this theatre season, the third edition of **"Mistero buffo"** is born (*Palazzina Liberty*, followed by tour).

In November opens at *Palazzina Liberty* a production of **"Tutta casa, letto e chiesa"** [**"Female parts"**], a piece mixing the grotesque, comic and dramatic to illustrate the situation of women today. Alone on the stage is Franca Rame, who for the first time puts her name besides Fo's on the author by-line. The performance is staged more than 3000 times.

It is in these years that Fo becomes Italy's most translated author. He is published in more than 50 countries and in more than 30 languages.

1979 Dario and Franca participate in the International Theatre Festival in Berlin with **"Mistero buffo"** and **"Tutta casa, letto e chiesa"**.

Fo writes **"La tragedia di Aldo Moro"**, on the kidnapping and assassination of the Italian Christian Democratic Party leader at the hands of the Red Brigades. The play, which has never been performed, is built on Sophocles' *Philoctetes*.

Re-elaborates and directs for Milan's La Scala Theatre "L'Histoire du Soldat" by Igor Stravinsky. Writes and directs **"Storia della tigre ['The Tale of the Tiger'] e altre storie"**.

1980 Franca, Dario and their son Jacopo found the *Libera Università di Alcatraz*, a cultural and agricultural retreat and study centre located in the hills between Gubbio and Perugia. By buying up, little by little, 3 700 000 square metres of forest (that otherwise would have been felled) and olive groves, the Fos prevent the destruction of a beautiful valley. They also restore eleven ancient and abandoned farm houses and medieval towers. Alcatraz becomes a gathering place for various artists and cultural groups — including Sergio Angese, Stefano Benni, Dacia Maraini, Milo Manara, Andrea Pazienza, Elena Cranco — who hold workshops in theatre, cartoon drawing, dance, writing, psychophysical techniques, psychology and craftsmanship. Alcatraz also arranges educational programmes and summer camps for young people, social outcasts and persons with handicap. The activities at the centre include equine therapy, comic therapy, nature walks and pool swimming including a swimming school. In addition, the centre offers natural gardening, an ecological restaurant and a facility to preserve organically grown fruit and produce. To date, the centre has had more than 3000 guests. It is directed by Jacopo Fo.

"**Buona sera con Franca Rame**" — by and with Fo– RAI 2 (20 shows).

March — Sweden: Stockholms Stadsteater (The City Theatre of Stockholm) stages **"Mistero buffo"** and **"Tutta casa, letto e chiesa"**.

May — Fo is invited by East Berlin's **Berliner Ensemble** to stage a production at Bertolt Brecht's prestigious theatre in the spring of 1981. Dario Fo prepares an adaptation of Brecht's "Three-penny Opera" that is rejected for its political content. The main resistance comes from Brecht's daughter (the Berlin Wall has not yet fallen). The same adaptation is used when the play is staged a year later at Turin's Teatro Stabile. Dario and Franca are invited to participate at the Italian Theatre Festival in New York. However, the US Department of State denies them entry visas to the United States. On 29 May, a large group of US artists and intellectuals organize a protest against the ruling. Among the protesters are Arthur Miller, Norman Mailer, Martin Scorsese, Ellen Stewart, Sol Yurrick, Eve Merriam and others.

December — France: Théâtre de L'Est Parisien stages **"Mistero Boffo"** and **"Tutta casa, letto e cbiesa"**.

Germany: Franca on stage with **"Tutta casa, letto e chiesa"** at the Volkshochschule in Frankfurt and the Deutsches Schauspielhaus in Bochum and in Hamburg.

1981 — The University of Copenhagen awards Fo with thc prestigious Sonning Prize, which he dedicates to Franca.

| | |
|---|---|
| 1981 | Franca in a production by RAI: "Mrs Warren's Profession" by G. B. Shaw, directed by Giorgio Albertazzi. |
| 1981–82 | **"Tutta casa, letto e chiesa"** in a new version, Milan's Odeon Theatre followed by tour. Franca writes **"Lo stupro"** and, with Dario, **"Una madre"** (about political prisoners), two monologues that are inserted in various performances.<br>Fo writes **"Clacson, trombette e pernacchi"** [**"Trumpets and raspberries"**], a comedy about terrorism. |
| 1982 | Turin's Teatro Stabile produces and Fo directs his new play **"L'Opera dello sghignazzo"**, a free adaptation of John Gay's "The Beggar's Opera", which also served as point of departure for Brecht's "Three-penny Opera". Dario Fo writes and produces **"Il fabulazzo osceno"**, based on **"Mistero boffo"** and **"Storia della tigre"**. With him on stage is Franca Rame who recites the two monologues **"Lo stupro"** and **"La madre"**.<br>London: Franca's performance of **"Tutta casa, letto e chiesa"** at the Riverside Studios is received with loud acclaim by critics and public alike. The same piece, in English translation ["Female Parts"], is performed by Yvonne Bryceland at the National Theatre.<br>Dario and Franca together write **"Coppia aperta"** [**"The Open Couple"**], which is immediately staged at Stockholm's famous Pistol Theatre, translated and directed by Anna and Carlo Barsotti. The play enjoys great success with critics and public. |
| 1983 May | London: Fo at the Riverside Studios with **"Mistero boffo"**.<br>Canada: Franca is invited to participate in the Festival Québéois du Jeune Théâtre with **"Tutta casa, letto e chiesa"**. |
| 1983–84 | Following the play's clamorous success in Sweden, Dario and Franca stage **"Coppia aperta"** with Nicola de Buono in the role of the husband (Teatro Ciak in |

| | |
|---|---|
| | Milan). The Ministerial Commission for Censorship bans the play to minors under 18 (!). The ruling is later recalled after protests from the press and the public. |
| January | Cuba: Festival de teatro de la Habana with **"Tutta casa, letto e cbiesa"**. |
| May | Argentina: Teatro Municipal General San Martín with **"Tutta casa, letto e chiesa"** and **"Mistero buffo"**. During a performance, a youth throws a military tear-gas grenade into the theatre. It explodes, creating panic among the audience of well over 1000 persons. Every evening throughout the stay in Argentina, young — and not so young — fascists in black leather jackets throw stones at the windows of the theatre — while tens of policemen stand by, watching complacently. Windows up to the third floor are broken. Meanwhile, groups of Catholics (instigated by fiery press articles by the Bishop of Buenos Aires, written before the arrival of the company), carrying oversized images of Jesus on their chests, pray in the lobby of the theatre. Others interrupt the performances with shouts every time the word "pope" was mentioned. These people are carried out of the theatre by the police. Reactions of support from authorities and the public, including the mothers of Plaza de Mayo.<br>Colombia: Teatro Colón with **"Tutta casa, letto e chiesa"** and **"Mistero buffo"**. |
| August | Franca and Dario at Edinburgh's Fringe Theatre Festival with **"Tutta casa, letto e chiesa"** and **"Mistero buffo"**.<br>Tour in Finland, Tampere: Festival of the Theatre of Dario Fo. Plays and performances by Fo–Rame are staged all over the city. Dario presents **"Mistero buffo"** and Franca **"Tutta casa, letto e chiesa"**.<br>They are invited by Joseph Papp to stage a production at New York's Public Theatre, but are denied entry into the USA for a second time.<br>Fo writes **"Patapunfete"**, a text for clowns, performed and directed by Ronald and Alfred Colombaioni. |

|  |  |
|---|---|
|  | During the summer, Fo writes **"Quasi per caso una donna: Elisabetta"** [**"Elizabeth: Almost by Chance a Woman"**], **"Dio li fa poi li accoppa"** and **"Lisistrata romana"**, the latter a monologue that has never been staged.<br>London: Riverside Studios with **"La storia della maschera"**.<br>Fo–Rame at Edinburgh's Fringe Theatre Festival. |
| 1984–85 | The first production of **"Quasi per caso una donna: Elisabetta"** opens in the autumn. The large number of people who come to see the play during the season earn Dario and Franca AGIS's "Golden Ticket" award. |
| May–June | Germany: The International Theatre Festival in Munich with **"Tutta casa, letto e chiesa"** and **"Mistero buffo"**. |
| May | Genua's Teatro della Tosse stages **"La vera storia di Piero d'Angera che allà crociata non c'era"**, directed by Tonino Conte, stage design and costumes by Lele Luzzati. |
| November | American producer Alexander Cohen stages a Broadway production of "Accidental Death of an Anarchist", with adaptations by Richard Nelsan, at New York's Belasco Theatre. The US Department of State finally — after personal intervention by President Reagan! — grants Fo and Rame a limited, six-day entry visa. |
| 1985–86 | For the Biennial exhibition in Venice, Fo writes and stages (with Rome University's Teatro Ateneo) **"Hellequin, Harlekin, Arlecchino"** at Venice's Palazzo del Cinema. He also writes **"Diario di Eva"** for Franca; but has yet to stage it. |
| September | Franca is invited to Copenhagen by the Danish actors' union to present a few of her monologues at a benefit performance. Franca visits Tübingen, Heidelberg, Stuttgart and Frankfurt with the Theater Am Turm to perform **"Coppia aperta"** with Giorgio Biavati. |
| May–June | USA: Dario and Franca are finally granted a normal entry visa for the United States. On the invitation of Harvard University, they perform **"Mistero boffo"** and **"Tutta casa, letto e chiesa"** at Cambridge's |

|  |  |
|---|---|
|  | American Repertory Theater, the New Haven University Repertory Theatre, Washington's Kennedy Center, Baltimore's Theater of Nations and New York's Joyce Theater. They hold a five-day theatre seminar at New York University as well as various workshops. Franca gives a lesson/performance at Wheaton College in Norton, Massachusetts. |
| August | Fo receives the Premio Eduardo from Taormina Arte. Franca at the Free Festival in Edinburgh with **"Coppia aperta"**. Participating in the festival are various companies presenting Fo–Rame texts in English translation: Yorick Theatre Co., Catwalk Theatre Productions, Fo–Rame Theatre Project, Warehouse Theatre, The Drama Department and Borderline Theatre. |
| 1986–87 | Franca opens at Milan's Teatro Nuovo with **"Parti fermminili"**, two one-act plays by Dario Fo and Franca Rame: **"Una giornata qualunque"** [**"An Ordinary Day"**] and an updated version of **"Coppia aperta"**. The same season sees the opening of **"Il ratto della Francesca"** with Franca Rame and others. |
| December | Pagani (Naples): Dario Fo receives the "Fifth national award against violence and the Camorra" from the Associazione Torre. |
| February | Dario Fo directs Rossini's "The Barber of Seville" at *De Nederlandse Opera* in Amsterdam. The same production — with another cast — is later staged at the Teatro Petruzzelli in Bari. |
| April | Dario and Franca are in Cambridge, Massachusetts, to direct "Archangels Don't Play Flipper" at the American Repertory Theatre. |
| June | In New York to receive the Obie Prize. |
| July | Franca Rame at the San Francisco Theater Festival with **"Coppia aperta"**. She holds a theatre workshop with well over a hundred participants, numbering actors, mimes, acrobats and magicians who have come from all parts of the United States to share experiences. |

| | |
|---|---|
| 1987–88 | At the Festival dell'Unità, before an audience of over 10 000, Dario Fo presents his piece **"La rava e la Cava"** (title later changed to **"La parte del leone"**), a tragicomic monologue on the political situation in Italy.
Franca Rame continues with **"Parti femminili"** and participates in a production for RAI 2, **"Una lepre con la faccia da bambina"**, a film by Gianni Sera on the ecological disaster in Seveso. In the meantime, Fo writes scripts for the eight episodes of **"Trasmissione forzata"** planned for RAI 3, where he also assumes the roles of director, costume designer, stage designer and actor (with Franca and others). Eleven more years have again passed since their last collaboration with RAI television.
They are awarded the Agro Dolce Prize in Campione d'Italia. |
| June | Franca tours Turin for RAI 2's production of **"Parti femminili"**. |
| 1988–89 | Franca Rame continues her Italian tour of **"Parti femminili"**. Fo has a film role in "Musica per vecchi animali", directed by Stefano Benni. |
| March | *De Nederlandse Opera* reopens with "The Barber of Seville", again directed by Fo. |
| 1989 | **"Lettera dalla Cina"** by Dario Fo staged at Milan's *Arco della Pace* and in other Italian cities as part of demonstrations against the events at Tienanmen Square. |
| May | Brazil: As part of the exhibition "Italia Viva", the Teatro Petruzzelli stages Fo's production of "The Barber of Seville" in São Paolo and Rio de Janeiro. In the same cities, Dario and Franca perform **"Mistero boffo"** and **"Parti femminili"** to a public already acquainted with their theatre through several productions by various Brazilian theatre companies. |
| 1989–90 | Fo writes two plays: **"Il braccato"**, a never-played piece with a Mafia theme, and **"Il papa e la strega"** [**"The Pope and the Witch"**], on the legalization of drugs. The latter is staged with Franca Rame, who thanks to |

| | |
|---|---|
| April–June | the large audience she reaches during the season again receives the "Golden ticket" award from AGIS. Paris: on the invitation of Antoine Vitez, Artistic Director of the *Comédie Française*, Fo stages Molière's "Le médecin malgré lui" and "Le médecin volant". Sadly, Vitez — who had fought to have Fo inaugurate his planned Molière cycle — is unable to witness the triumphs that the productions reap with critics and public alike. He passes away towards the end of April. Fo is the first Italian director to stage a production at the *Comédie Française*. Among the spectators is President Mitterrand, who praises the productions in a personal letter to Dario Fo. |
| May | Fo is invited by the Berliner Ensemble to stage a production in Bertolt Brecht's old theatre in the spring of 1991. The project is never finalized. |
| July | Franca Rame films **"Coppia aperta"** for Swiss national television. |
| 1990–91 | Fo writes and produces at Milan's Teatro Nuovo **"Zitti! Stiamo precipitando!"**, a comic-grotesque farce about AIDS. The piece — with Dario Fo, Franca Rame and others on stage — is played at many of the country's major theatres. In several cities, it is alternated with **"Mistero buffo"**, always in high demand.<br>The open-ended structure of **"Mistero buffo"** allows it to evolve over the years, permitting Fo to address the various issues which over time attract his interest and that of the public. |
| April | As part of the Eleventh International Theatre Festival, Dario and Franca stage **"Mistero bufro"** in Palma and Seville. |
| May | Fo is invited to participate with a new production at Seville's 1992 World Exhibition on the occasion of the fifth anniversary of the discovery of America. |
| May | Fo's production of "The Barber of Seville" at *De Nederlandse Opera* is filmed by Dutch national television. |

| | |
|---|---|
| 1991–92 | Dario Fo on stage with his new monologue **"Johan Padan a la descoverta de le Americhe"**. The text is the fruit of his research on the lives of a group of Europeans shipwrecked in the early 16th Century. Using testimonials recovered from that time, Fo tells the story — in a reinvented, antique language — of a group of Mississippi Indians resisting the European incursion. This five centuries old struggle marks the beginning of the undefeated Seminole nation's fight for its survival, an epic story that from the beginning has been censored from the pages of history. |
| October | Dario and Franca at the Italian Theatre festival in Moscow, organized by the Russian Writers' Association and ETI. They stage **"Mistero burro"** at the Taganka Theatre. |
| April | Spain: the Centro Dramatico in Valencia puts on a production of Fo's 1962 play **"Isabella, tre caravelle e un cacciaballe"**, slightly revised on occasion of the "celebration" of the quincentennial anniversary of the "discovery" of America.<br>Fo participates with **"Johan Padan"** in the World Exhibition in Seville in 1992.<br>**"Parliamo di donne"**, consisting of two one-act pieces (**"L'Eroina"** and **"Grassa è bello"**), is staged in September at Milan's Teatro Nuovo. The pieces are written with Franca Rame who also plays the leading roles. **"L'Eroina"** tells the tragic story of a mother of three drug-addicted children, of which one dies of an overdose and another of AIDS. To save the life of the third child, the mother prostitutes herself to afford to keep him with drugs: "A drug addiction can be cured but AIDS can only kill". In **"Grassa è bello"**, Franca — in a foam rubber body suit to make her look grossly overweight — airs thoughts on femininity, what it means to be sexy, slimming, dieting, love and life in general. As often happens when Franca is on stage, several performances are cancelled because the theatre owners get cold feet following a bigoted press campaign. |

| | |
|---|---|
| June | Fo directs a new production of "The Barber of Seville", this time for the Paris Opera playing at the *Opéra Garnier*. |
| October | *De Nederlandse Opera* opens with "The Barber of Seville" for yet another season.
Also continuing for another season are Fo's productions of Molière's "Le médecin malgré lui" and "Le médecin volant" at the *Comédie Française*. |
| 1992–93 | **"Settimo: ruba un po' meno! n. 2"** by Dario Fo and Franca Rame. In this one-act play, staged as the floodgates of the wide-reaching graft scandal known in Italy as "*tangentopoli*" ["bribe city"] opened, Franca Rame talks in simple terms about the thievery that has become custom in Italy's political establishment. No embellishments are necessary for dramatic effects. |
| July 1993 | At the Festival dei Due Mondi in Spoleto, Franca Rame and others read **"Dario Fo incontra Ruzzante"**. |
| 1993–94 | Dario Fo writes and plays in **"Mamma! I sanculotti!"**, a piece that, in the tradition of comic theatre, through dance, mime and song, tells the story of a public prosecutor who investigates graft and corruption in and out of Parliament. |
| 1994 | **"Un palcoscenico per le donne"**: At Milan's Porta Romana Theatre, Franca Rame organizes a theatrical review, by and for women, with young playwright/actresses. In August, the review is played in Cesenatico with great success. |
| April | Franca: a new season with **"Settimo: ruba un po' meno n. 2"**. |
| May | In cooperation with the Municipality of Cervia, Franca organizes a performance for a group of Italian and foreign actors and actresses. Participants come from Denmark, the United Kingdom, the United States and Turkey. |
| August | At the Rossini Opera Festival in Pesaro, Fo directs Rossini's "L'Italiana in Algeri". |
| 1994–95 | In October, Franca opens in Milan with **"Sesso? grazie, tanto per gradire!"**, by Franca Rame and Jacopo and Dario Fo, based on Jacopo Fo's book *Lo* |

*zen e l'arte di scopare* (more than 300 000 copies sold). In the grotesque and ironic text, Franca Rame — departing from her own first sexual experiences — illustrates how we are kept in the dark as we grow up, with the idea that sexuality — above all women's sexuality — is something indecent. At first, the Ministerial Commission for Censorship bans the performance for minors under 18 years. After two months of press campaigns and litigation, the ban is dropped, and the performance is described as "brimming with profound maternal love and therefore recommended to minors".

December   Fo's production of Rossini's "L'Italiana in Algeri" is staged at *De Nederlandse Opera* to resounding international acclaim. The production is filmed by Dutch national television.

Franca visits Toronto with an enthusiastically received performance of **"Sesso? Grazie, tanto per gradire!"**.

January   Dario Fo opens in Florence with **"Dario Fo recita Ruzzante"**, a satirical monologue and an homage to Angelo Beolco. The text is an elaboration of the one already read at the Festival in Spoleto, enriched with new material. The performance meets with unanimous praise from Italy's theatre critics and draws a large audience.

Walter Valeri, who manages the Fo–Rame company's foreign bookings, prepares an international tour in France, the United Kingdom, Germany and the United States. Scheduled for the tour are performances of **"Johan Padan a la scoperta de le Americhe"** and **"Sesso? Grazie, tanto per gradire!"**, as well as seminars at leading universities with central figures in American theatre.

On 17 July, Dario is struck by cerebral ischaemia and loses 80 percent of his sight. All plans are put on hold. In order to honour commitments to technical and administrative personnel, Franca Rame continues in the autumn with her Italian tour of **"Sesso? Grazie, tanto per gradire!"**, while Dario rests and recuperates. His condition is good and improves day by day.

| | |
|---|---|
| 1996–97 | Dario begins to reassume his tasks: he holds classes in theatre schools and at universities, and gives a special performance of **"Arlecchino"** at Venice's Teatro Goldoni. |
| July | He writes **"Bibbia dei villani"** for the festival of Benevento. The performance is staged in September. |
| May | Dario and Franca visit Copenhagen, where they hold an open seminar at Folkteatret. Franca arranges a theatre evening with Danish actresses and gives performances of **"Sesso? Grazie, tanto per gradire!"**. The couple also inaugurates an exhibition of their drawings, costumes and puppets at the National Museum.

In the autumn, Dario and Franca continue with their Italian tour of **"Mistero buffo"** and **"Sesso? Grazie, tanto per gradire!"**, merging the two pieces into a single performance played at major theatres as well as sports arenas before large audiences (up to 5000 people). In order not to tire Dario too much, the activities of the company are otherwise reduced.

During this tour, Dario and Franca write **"Il diavolo con le Zinne"**, a comic–grotesque spectacle that for its richness and variety in language, its theatrical invention and its elements of song and dance, is best described as an opera. It is a great success.

Dario is now cured of his illness, and his eyesight has improved so much that Franca gives him a computerized typewriter (he refuses to use a computer). They are very happy! |
| 1997–98 | For the Festival of Taormina, CTFR, GIGA and Taormina Arte produce **"Il diavolo con le zinne"**, directed by Dario Fo, who also designs costumes and décor. On stage are Franca Rame and Giorgio Albertazzi. The play opens on 7 August 1997 at the Teatro Vittorio Emanuele in Messina.

The production continues the following season and is taken on tour throughout Italy, where it meets with great success. |

**9 October 1997 Dario Fo receives the Nobel Prize in literature.**
1999   He publishes **"Lu Santo Jullàre Francesco"** and **"La vera storia di Ravenna"**.

PLAYS DIRECTED BY DARIO FO AND FRANCA RAME

1962 GLI AMICI DELLA BATTONIERA — Teatro Ridotto, Venice
1963 CHI RUBA UN PIEDE È FORTUNATO IN AMORE — Lilla Teatern, Helsinki
1967 LA PASSEGGIATA DELLA DOMENICA — by M. Archard, translation and arrangement by Dario Fo; Teatro Durini, Milan
1968 ENZO JANNACCI: 22 CANZONI — Teatro Odeon, Milan
1978 LA STORIA DI UN SOLDATO (L'HISTOIRE DU SOLDAT) — by I. Stravinsky; Teatro alla Scala, Milan
1981 L'OPERA DELLO SGHIGNAZZO — elaboration of "The Beggar's Opera" by J. Gay; Teatro Stabile, Turin
1986 TUTTA CASA, LETTO E CHIESA — Belgium and France
1987 THE BARBER OF SEVILLE — by Go Rossini; De Nederlandse Opera, Amsterdam
1987 ARCHANGELS DON'T PLAY FLIPPER — American Repertory Theater, Cambridge (Mass.)
1988 THE BARBER OF SEVILLE — by G. Rossini; Teatro Petruzzelli, Bari
1989 THE BARBER OF SEVILLE — by G. Rossini; tour with Teatro Petruzzelli in Brazil (São Paolo and Rio de Janeiro)
1990 LE MÉDECIN MALGRÉ LUI/LE MÉDECIN VOIANT — by Molière; Comédie Française, Paris
1990 THE BARBER OF SEVILLE — by G. Rossini; De Nederlandse Opera, Amsterdam
1991 IL MEDICO PER FORZA/IL MEDICO VOLANTE — by Molière; Comédie Française, Paris
1992 ISABELLA, TRE CARAVELLE E UN CACCIABALLE — Centro Dramatico Nacional, Valencia
1992 THE BARBER OF SEVILLE — by G. Rossini; De Nederlandse Opera, Amsterdam (filmed for Dutch TV)
1992 THE BARBER OF SEVILLE — by G. Rossini; Opera Garnier, Paris

| | |
|---|---|
| 1994 | L'ITALIANA IN ALGERI — by G. Rossini; Pesaro Opera Festival, Pesaro |
| 1994 | THE BARBER OF SEVILLE — by G. Rossini; De Nederlandse Opera, Amsterdam |
| 1996 | THE BARBER OF SEVILLE — by G. Rossini; Israel (produced by Arturo Corso) |
| 1997 | THE BARBER OF SEVILLE — by G. Rossini; Sweden (staged by Carlo Barsotti) |

WORK IN FILM AND TELEVISION

| | |
|---|---|
| 1952 | PAPAVERI E PAPERE, a film by Marcello Marchesi with Franca Rame and Walter Chiari. |
| 1956 | MONETINE DA 5 LIRE, a television comedy by Dario Fo for RAI. |
| 1956 | LO SVITATO, a film by Carlo Lizzani with Franca Rame, script by Dario Fo. |
| 1961 | CHI L'HA VISTO?, a television series for RAI 2 (6 episodes). |
| 1962 | CANZONISSIMA, a television series for RAI 1 (13 episodes). Fo writes the texts, directs and — with Franca Rame — hosts the show, which is one of the most popular on Italian television. Due to the political content of some of the sketches, the show is censured. Dario Fo and Franca Rame leave the show in protest. As a consequence, they are sued by RAI's management which bans them from television for 15 years. |
| 1976 | FANFANI RAPITO, film. |
| 1977 | IL TEATRO DI DARIO FO, seven televised comedies by and with Dario Fo and Franca Rame, for RAI 2. |
| 1978 | BUONASERA CON FRANCA RAME, a television series for RAI 2 (20 episodes). |
| 1978 | PARLIAMO DI DONNE, 2 episodes with Franca Rame. |
| 1981 | MRS WARREN'S PROFESSION by G. B. Shaw, directed for television by G. Albertazzi, with Franca Rame. |
| 1988 | TRASMISSIONE FORZATA with Dario Fo and Franca Rame, for RAI 3. |
| 1989 | UNA LEPRE CON LA FACCIA DA BAMBINA, film for television by G. Serra, with Franca Rame. |
| 1989 | UNA GIORNATA QUALUNQUE and COPPIA APERTA for RAI 2, with Franca Rame. |

1989    PROMESSI SPOSI, Dario Fo.
1989    MUSICA PER VECCHI ANIMALI, film for television by S. Benni, with Dario Fo.
1990    COPPIA APERTA, Swiss national television, with Franca Rame.
1991    SETTIMO: RUBA UN PO' MENO, for RAI 2.
1991    MISTERO BUFFO, for RAI 2, with Dario Fo and Franca Rame.
1993    RUZZANTE, for RAI 2.

COUNTRIES IN WHICH THE THEATRE OF DARIO FO AND FRANCA RAME HAS BEEN PLAYED

| | | |
|---|---|---|
| Argentina | Greenland | Poland |
| Australia | Hungary | Portugal |
| Austria | Iceland | Puerto Rico |
| Belgium | India | Romania |
| Brazil | Ireland | Scotland |
| Bulgaria | Israel | Singapore |
| Canada | Japan | South Africa |
| Chile | Keny | Spain |
| China | Luxembourg | Sweden |
| Colombia | Malta | Switzerland |
| Czechoslovakia | Mexico | Turkey |
| Denmark | Monaco | South Korea |
| England | The Netherlands | Soviet Union |
| Estonia | New Guinea | United States |
| Finland | New Zealand | Uruguay |
| France | Norway | Venezuela |
| Germany | Paraguay | Yugoslavia |
| Greece | Peru | Zimbabwe |

## CITIES HOSTING EXHIBITS OF THE THEATRE OF DARIO FO AND FRANCA RAME

ITALY: Bergamo, Cesena, Forlì, Milan, Palermo, Pesaro, Riccione, Venice
SPAIN: Barcelona, Madrid
DENMARK: Copenhagen
FINLAND: Helsinki

The NETHERLANDS: Amsterdam

The exhibits contain paintings, masks, hand- and string-puppets, tapestries, sketches for stage design, stage machinery, direction notes and costumes.

*Translated by Paul Claesson*

# CONTRA JOGULATORES OBLOQUENTES
# AGAINST JESTERS WHO DEFAME AND INSULT

Nobel Lecture, December 7, 1997
by
DARIO FO
Milan, Italy

> "Against jesters who defame and insult." Law issued by emperor Frederick II (Messina 1221), declaring that anyone may commit violence against jesters without incurring punishment or sanction.

The drawings I'm showing you are mine. Copies of these, slightly reduced in size, have been distributed among you.

For some time it's been my habit to use images when preparing a speech; rather than write it down, I illustrate it. This allows me to improvise, to exercise my imagination — and to oblige you to use yours.

As I proceed, I will from time to time indicate to you where we are in the manuscript. That way you won't lose the thread. This will be of help especially to those of you who don't understand either Italian or Swedish. English-speakers will have a tremendous advantage over the rest because they will imagine things I've neither said nor thought. There is of course the problem of the two laughters: those who understand Italian will laugh immediately, those who don't will have to wait for Anna [Barsotti]'s Swedish translation. And then there are those of you who won't know whether to laugh the first time or the second. Anyway, let's get started.

Ladies and gentlemen, the title I've selected for this little chat is "contra jogulatores obloquentes", which you all recognize as Latin, mediaeval Latin to be precise. It's the title of a law issued in Sicily in 1221 by Emperor Frederick II of Swabia, an emperor "anointed by God", who we were taught in school to regard as a sovereign of extraordinary enlightenment, a liberal. "Jogulatores obloquentes" means "jesters who defame and insult". The law in question allowed any and all citizens to insult jesters, to beat them and even — if they were in that mood — to kill them, without running any risk of being brought to trial and condemned. I hasten to assure you that this law no longer is in vigour, so I can safely continue.

*Ladies and gentlemen,*
Friends of mine, noted men of letters, have in various radio and television interviews declared: "The highest prize should no doubt be awarded to the members of the Swedish Academy, for having had the courage this year to award the Nobel Prize to a jester." I agree. Yours is an act of courage that borders on provocation.

It's enough to take stock of the uproar it has caused: sublime poets and writers who normally occupy the loftiest of spheres, and who rarely take interest in those who live and toil on humbler planes, are suddenly bowled over by some kind of whirlwind.

Like I said, I applaud and concur with my friends.

These poets had already ascended to the Parnassian heights when you, through your insolence, sent them toppling to earth, where they fell face and belly down in the mire of normality.

Insults and abuse are hurled at the Swedish Academy, at its members and their relatives back to the seventh generation. The wildest of them clamour: "Down with the King ... of Norway!". It appears they got the dynasty wrong in the confusion.

(At this point you may turn the page. As you see there is an image of a naked poet bowled over by a whirlwind.)

Some landed pretty hard on their nether parts. There were reports of poets and writers whose nerves and livers suffered terribly. For a few days thereafter there was not a pharmacy in Italy that could muster up a single tranquillizer.

But, dear members of the Academy, let's admit it, this time you've overdone it. I mean come on, first you give the prize to a black man, then to a Jewish writer. Now you give it to a clown. What gives? As they say in Naples: *pazziàmme?* Have we lost our senses?

Also the higher clergy have suffered their moments of madness. Sundry potentates — great electors of the Pope, bishops, cardinals and prelates of Opus Dei — have all gone through the ceiling, to the point that they've even petitioned for the reinstatement of the law that allowed jesters to be burned at the stake. Over a slow fire.

On the other hand, I can tell you there is an extraordinary number of people who rejoice with me over your choice. And so I bring you the most festive thanks, in the name of a multitude of mummers, jesters, clowns, tumblers and storytellers.

(This is where we are now [indicates a page].)

And speaking of storytellers, I mustn't forget those of the small town on Lago Maggiore where I was born and raised, a town with a rich oral tradition.

They were the old storytellers, the master glass-blowers who taught me and other children the craftsmanship, the art, of spinning fantastic yarns. We would listen to them, bursting with laughter — laughter that would stick in our throats as the tragic allusion that surmounted each sarcasm would dawn on us. To this day I keep fresh in my mind the story of the Rock of Caldé.

"Many years ago", began the old glass-blower, "way up on the crest of that steep cliff that rises from the lake there was a town called Caldé. As it happened, this town was sitting on a loose splinter of rock that slowly, day by day, was sliding down towards the precipice. It was a splendid little town, with a campanile, a fortified tower at the very peak and a cluster of houses, one after the other. It's a town that once was and that now is gone. It disappeared in the 15th century.

"'Hey', shouted the peasants and fishermen down in the valley below. 'You're sliding, you'll fall down from there'.

"But the cliff dwellers wouldn't listen to them, they even laughed and made fun of them: 'You think you're pretty smart, trying to scare us into running away from our houses and our land so you can grab them instead. But we're not that stupid.'

"So they continued to prune their vines, sow their fields, marry and make love. They went to mass. They felt the rock slide under their houses but they didn't think much about it. 'Just the rock settling. Quite normal', they said, reassuring each other.

"The great splinter of rock was about to sink into the lake. 'Watch out, you've got water up to your ankles', shouted the people along the shore. 'Nonsense, that's just drainage water from the fountains, it's just a bit humid', said the people of the town, and so, slowly but surely, the whole town was swallowed by the lake.

"Gurgle ... gurgle ... splash ... they sink ... houses, men, women, two horses, three donkeys ... heehaw ... gurgle. Undaunted, the priest continued to receive the confession of a nun: 'Te absolvi ... animus ... santi ... guurgle ... Aame ... gurgle ...' The tower disappeared, the campanile sank with bells and all: Dong ... ding ... dop ... plock ...

"Even today", continued the old glass-blower, "if you look down into the water from that outcrop that still juts out from the lake, and if in that same moment a thunderstorm breaks out, and the lightning illuminates the bottom of the lake, you can still see — incredible as it may seem! — the submerged town, with its streets still intact and even the inhabitants themselves, walking around and glibly repeating to themselves: 'Nothing has happened'. The fish swim back and forth before their eyes, even into their ears. But they just brush them off: 'Nothing to worry about. It's just some kind of fish that's learned to swim in the air'.

"'Atchoo!' 'God bless you!' 'Thank you ... it's a bit humid today ... more than yesterday ... but everything's fine'. They've reached rock bottom, but as far as they're concerned, nothing has happened at all."

Disturbing though it may be, there's no denying that a tale like this still has something to tell us.

I repeat, I owe much to these master glass-blowers of mine, and they — I assure you — are immensely grateful to you, members of this Academy, for rewarding one of their disciples.

And they express their gratitude with explosive exuberance. In my home town, people swear that on the night the news arrived that one of their own storytellers was to be awarded the Nobel Prize, a kiln that had been standing cold for some fifty years suddenly erupted in a broadside of flames, spraying high into the air — like a fireworks *finale* — a myriad splinters of coloured glass, which then showered down on the surface of the lake, releasing an impressive cloud of steam.

(While you applaud, I'll have a drink of water. [Turning to the interpreter:] Would you like some?

It's important that you talk among yourselves while we drink, because if you try to hear the gurgle gurgle gurgle the water makes as we swallow we'll choke on it and start coughing. So instead you can exchange niceties like "Oh, what a lovely evening it is, isn't it?".

End of intermission: we turn to a new page, but don't worry, it'll go faster from here.)

Above all others, this evening you're due the loud and solemn thanks of an extraordinary master of the stage, little-known not only to you and to people in France, Norway, Finland ... but also to the people of Italy. Yet he was, until Shakespeare, doubtless the greatest playwright of renaissance Europe. I'm referring to Ruzzante Beolco, my greatest master along with Molière: both actors-playwrights, both mocked by the leading men of letters of their times. Above all, they were despised for bringing onto the stage the everyday life, joys and desperation of the common people; the hypocrisy and the arrogance of the high and mighty; and the incessant injustice. And their major, unforgivable fault was this: in telling these things, they made people laugh. Laughter does not please the mighty.

Ruzzante, the true father of the *Commedia dell'Arte*, also constructed a language of his own, a language of and for the theatre, based on a variety of tongues: the dialects of the Po Valley, expressions in Latin, Spanish, even German, all mixed with onomatopoeic sounds of his own invention. It is from him, from Beolco Ruzzante, that I've learned to free myself from conventional literary writing and to express myself with words that you can chew, with unusual sounds, with various techniques of rhythm and breathing, even with the rambling nonsense-speech of the *grammelot*.

Allow me to dedicate a part of this prestigious prize to Ruzzante.

A few days ago, a young actor of great talent said to me: "Maestro, you should try to project your energy, your enthusiasm, to young people. You have to give them this charge of yours. You have to share your professional knowledge and experience with them". Franca — that's my wife — and I looked at each other and said: "He's right". But when we teach others our art, and share this charge of fantasy, what end will it serve? Where will it lead?

In the past couple of months, Franca and I have visited a number of university campuses to hold workshops and seminars before young audiences. It has been surprising — not to say disturbing — to discover their ignorance about the times we live in. We told them about the proceedings now in course in Turkey against the accused culprits of the massacre in Sivas. Thirty-seven of the country's foremost democratic intellectuals, meeting in the Anatolian town to celebrate the memory of a famous mediaeval jester of the Ottoman period, were burned alive in the dark of the night, trapped inside their hotel. The fire was the handiwork of a group of fanatical fundamentalists that enjoyed protection from elements within the Government itself. In one night, thirty-seven of the country's most celebrated artists, writers, directors, actors and Kurdish dancers were erased from this Earth.

In one blow these fanatics destroyed some of the most important exponents of Turkish culture.

Thousands of students listened to us. The looks in their faces spoke of their astonishment and incredulity. They had never heard of the massacre. But what impressed me the most is that not even the teachers and professors present had heard of it. There Turkey is, on the Mediterranean, practically in front of us, insisting on joining the European Community, yet no one had heard of the massacre. Salvini, a noted Italian democrat, was right on the mark when he observed: "The widespread ignorance of events is the main buttress of injustice". But this absent-mindedness on the part of the young has been conferred upon them by those who are charged to educate and inform them: among the absent-minded and uninformed, school teachers and other educators deserve first mention.

Young people easily succumb to the bombardment of gratuitous banalities and obscenities that each day is served to them by the mass media: heartless TV action films where in the space of ten minutes they are treated to three rapes, two assassinations, one beating and a serial crash involving ten cars on a bridge that then collapses, whereupon everything — cars, drivers and passengers — precipitates into the sea ... only one person survives the fall, but he doesn't know how to swim and so drowns, to the cheers of the crowd of curious onlookers that suddenly has appeared on the scene.

At another university we spoofed the project — alas well under way — to manipulate genetic material, or more specifically, the proposal by the European Parliament to allow patent rights on living organisms. We could feel how the subject sent a chill through the audience. Franca and I explained how our Eurocrats, kindled by powerful and ubiquitous multinationals, are preparing a scheme worthy the plot of a sci-fi/horror movie entitled "Frankenstein's pig brother". They're trying to get the approval of a directive which (and get this!) would authorize industries to take patents on living beings, or on parts of them, created with techniques of genetic manipulation that seem taken straight out of "The Sorcerer's Apprentice".

This is how it would work: by manipulating the genetic make-up of a pig, a scientist succeeds in making the pig more human-like. By this arrangement it becomes much easier to remove from the pig the organ of your choice — a liver, a kidney — and to transplant it in a human. But to assure that the transplanted pig-organs aren't rejected, it's also necessary to transfer certain pieces of genetic information from the pig to the human. The result: a human pig (even though you will say that there are already plenty of those).

And every part of this new creature, this humanized pig, will be subject to patent laws; and whosoever wishes a part of it will have to pay copyright fees to the company that "invented" it. Secondary illnesses, monstrous deformations, infectious diseases — all are optionals, included in the price ...

The Pope has forcefully condemned this monstrous genetic witchcraft. He has called it an offence against humanity, against the dignity of man, and has gone to pains to underscore the project's total and irrefutable lack of moral value.

The astonishing thing is that while this is happening, an American scientist, a remarkable magician — you've probably read about him in the papers — has succeeded in transplanting the head of a baboon. He cut the heads off two baboons and switched them. The baboons didn't feel all that great after the operation. In fact, it left them paralysed, and they both died shortly thereafter, but the experiment worked, and that's the great thing.

But here's the rub: this modern-day Frankenstein, a certain Professor White, is all the while a distinguished member of the Vatican Academy of Sciences. Somebody should warn the Pope.

So, we enacted these criminal farces to the kids at the universities, and they laughed their heads off. They would say of Franca and me: "They're a riot, they come up with the most fantastic stories". Not for a moment, not even with an inkling in their spines, did they grasp that the stories we told were true.

These encounters have strengthened us in our conviction that our job is — in keeping with the exhortation of the great Italian poet Savinio — "to tell our own story". Our task as intellectuals, as persons who mount the pulpit or the stage, and who, most importantly, address to young people, our task is not just to teach them method, like how to use the arms, how to control breathing, how to use the stomach, the voice, the falsetto, the *contraccampo*. It's not enough to teach a technique or a style: we have to show them what is happening around us. They have to be able to tell their own story. A theatre, a literature, an artistic expression that does not speak for its own time has no relevance.

Recently, I took part in a large conference with lots of people where I tried to explain, especially to the younger participants, the ins and outs of a particular Italian court case. The original case resulted in seven separate proceedings, at the end of which three Italian left-wing politicians were sentenced to 21 years of imprisonment each, accused of having murdered a police commissioner. I've studied the documents of the case — as I did when I prepared *Accidental Death of an Anarchist* — and at the conference I recounted the facts pertaining to it, which are really quite absurd, even farcical. But at a certain point I realized I was speaking to deaf ears, for the simple reason that my audience was ignorant not only of the case itself, but of what had happened five years earlier, ten years earlier: the violence, the terrorism. They knew nothing about the massacres that occurred in Italy, the trains that blew up, the bombs in the *piazze* or the farcical court cases that have dragged on since then.

The terribly difficult thing is that in order to talk about what is happening today, I have to start with what happened thirty years ago and then work my way forward. It's not enough to speak about the present. And pay attention, this isn't just about Italy: the same thing happens everywhere, all over Europe. I've tried in Spain and encountered the same difficulty; I've tried in France, in Germany, I've yet to try in Sweden, but I will.

To conclude, let me share this medal with Franca.

Franca Rame, my companion in life and in art who you, members of the Academy, acknowledge in your motivation of the prize as actress and author; who has had a hand in many of the texts of our theatre.

(At this very moment, Franca is on stage in a theatre in Italy but will join me the day after tomorrow. Her flight arrives midday, if you like we can all head out together to pick her up at the airport.)

Franca has a very sharp wit, I assure you. A journalist put the following question to her: "So how does it feel to be the wife of a Nobel Prize winner? To have a monument in your home?" To which she answered: "I'm not worried. Nor do I feel at all at a disadvantage; I've been in training for a long time. I do my exercises each morning: I go down on my hand and knees, and that way I've accustomed myself to becoming a pedestal to a monument. I'm pretty good at it."

Like I said, she has a sharp wit. At times she even turns her irony against herself.

Without her at my side, where she has been for a lifetime, I would never have accomplished the work you have seen fit to honour. Together we've staged and recited thousands of performances, in theatres, occupied factories, at university sit-ins, even in deconsecrated churches, in prisons and city parks, in sunshine and pouring rain, always together. We've had to endure abuse, assaults by the police, insults from the right-thinking, and violence. And it is Franca who has had to suffer the most atrocious aggression. She has had to pay more dearly than any one of us, with her neck and limb in the balance, for the solidarity with the humble and the beaten that has been our premise.

The day it was announced that I was to be awarded the Nobel Prize I found myself in front of the theatre on Via di Porta Romana in Milan where Franca, together with Giorgio Albertazzi, was performing *The Devil with Tits*. Suddenly I was surrounded by a throng of reporters, photographers and camera-wielding TV-crews. A passing tram stopped, unexpectedly, the driver stepped out to greet me, then all the passengers stepped out too, they applauded me, and everyone wanted to shake my hand and congratulate me ... when at a certain point they all stopped in their tracks and, as with a single voice, shouted "Where's Franca?". They began to holler "Francaaa" until, after a little while, she appeared. Discombobulated and moved to tears, she came down to embrace me.

At that moment, as if out of nowhere, a band appeared, playing nothing but wind instruments and drums. It was made up of kids from all parts of the city and, as it happened, they were playing together for the first time. They struck up "Porta Romana bella, Porta Romana" in samba beat. I've never heard anything played so out of tune, but it was the most beautiful music Franca and I had ever heard.

Believe me, this prize belongs to both of us.

Thank you

*Translated by Paul Claesson*

CONTRA JOGULATORES OBLOQUENTES

AMICI
LETTERATI
ARTISTI
FAMOSI

MEMBRI DELL'ACCADEMIA

INTERVISTA

GIULLARE

PROVOCAZIONE
PUTIFERIO

PARNASO DEGLI ELETTI 2

POETI E PENSATORI SUBLIMI
CHE VOLANO ALTO
TRAVOLTI
DA UNA TROMBA D'ARIA
IMPROPERI TREMENDI AI MEMBRI
ABBASSO IL RE DI NORVEGIA

3
MA CHE?
PAZIAMMO?
LA CURIA È IMPAZZITA
TEATRANTI
HANNO
STRAGIOITO

GUITTI
GIULLARI
CLOWN
SALTIMBANCHI
FABULATORI DEL LAGO
FAVOLE ASSURDE CHE NOI RAGAZZI
COMMENTAVAMO CON SGHIGNAZZI

SILENZI PER LA TRAGICA 5
ALLEGORIA

TANTI ANNI FA
RACCONTAVA IL
MAESTRO SOFFIATORE

STAVA
ARROCCATO
UN PAESE
DI NOME
CALDE'

CHE GIORNO DOPO GIORNO
FRANAVA TUTTO IN BLOCCO

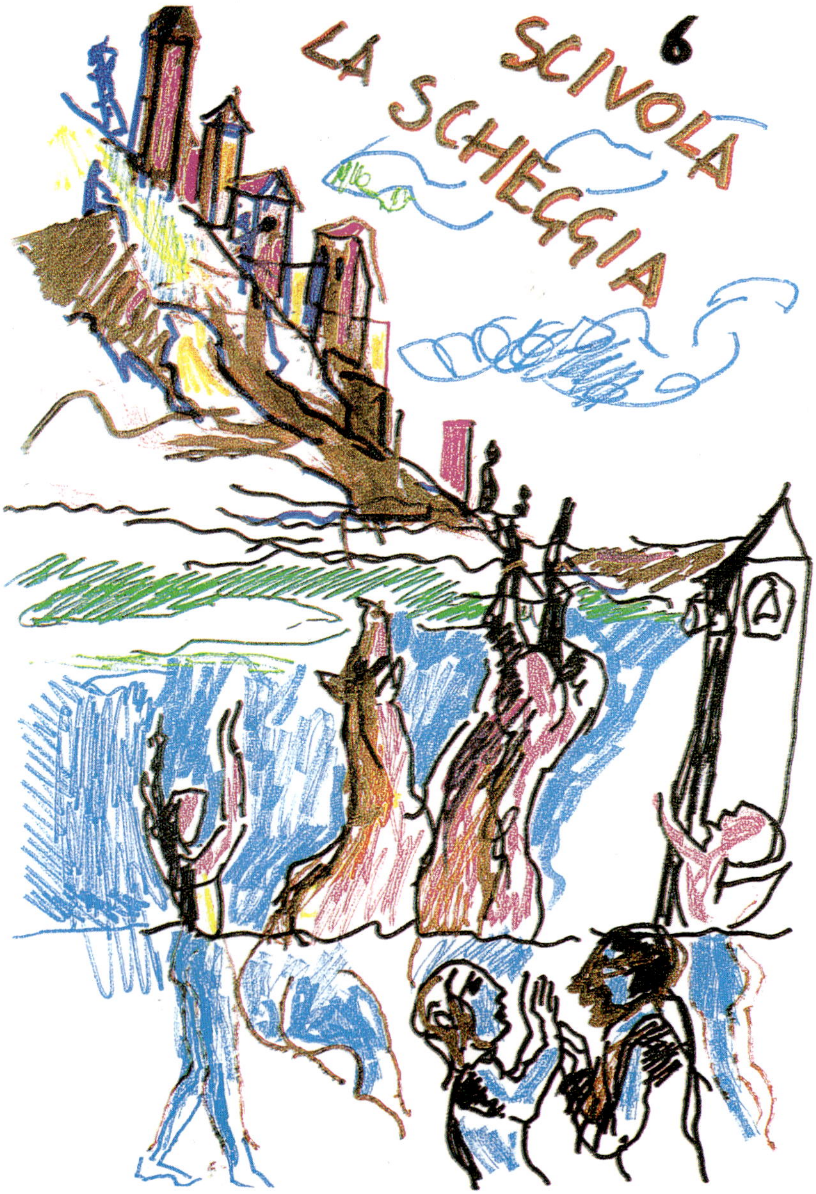
6
SCIVOLA
LA SCHEGGIA

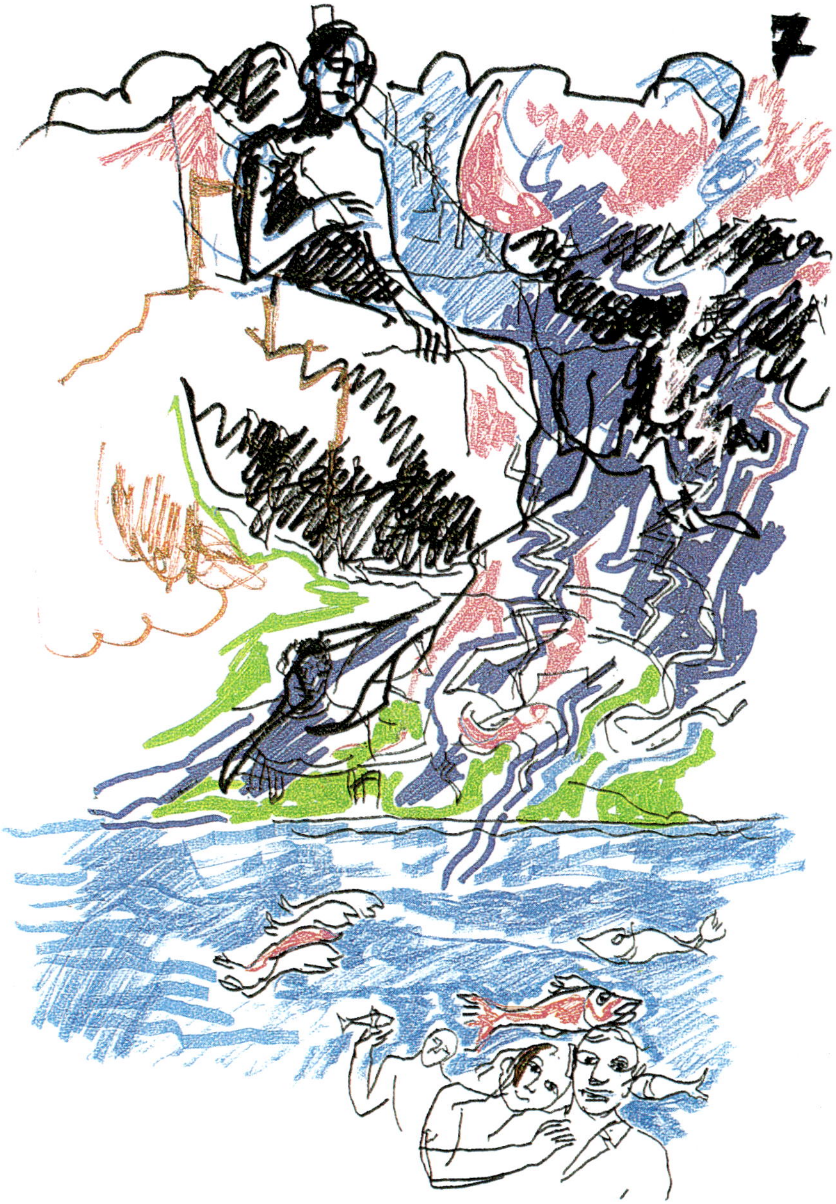

PERSONALMENTE
8
IO DEVO MOLTO AI MAESTRI
SOFFIATORI
FOLLEMENTE
ESPLOSIVO

SI LEVA SOLENNE E' FRAGOROSO IL SALUTO

RUZZANTE

SHAKESPEARE
MOLIÈRE

ENTRAMBI DISPREZZATI DAI SACCENTI

10° PADRE DEI COMICI DELL'ARTE

LESSICO IDIOMI

PROIETTARE L'ENERGIA AI GIOVANI

INSIEME ALL'UNIVERSITÀ

# TURCHIA 11

## STRAGE DI SIVAS

### IN ANATOLIA

**37**

SCRITTORI AUTORI ATTORI DANZATRICI RITO CURDO

ASCOLTAVANO INCREDULI 12
IGNORANZA DEL NOSTRO TEMPO

SAVINIO
L'IGNORANZA DIFFUSA DEI FATTI E' IL MAGGIOR SUPPORTO ALL' INGIUSTIZIA

L'ASSENZA -   IL SILENZIO

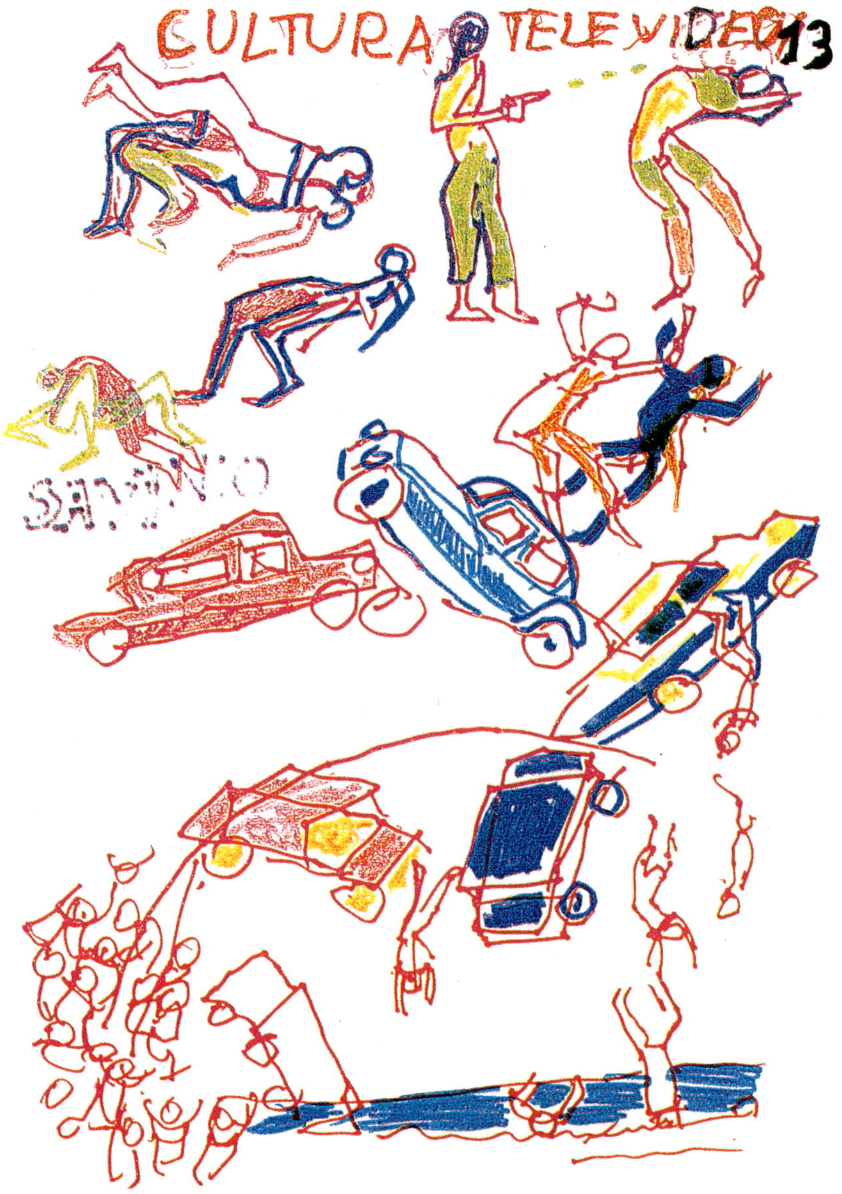
CULTURA
13

14
PROGETTO: BREVETTARE
ORGA-
NISMI
VIVENTI
FRATELLO
PORCO DI
FRANKESTEIN
MANIPOLAZIONE
GENETICA

15
METTERE LE MANI NEL
CORREDOGENETICO DI UN
MAIALE
RIESCE
A RENDERLO
FEGATO
RENE
DA TRAPIANTO

SENI PARTICELLE AVREMO L'UOMO MAIALE

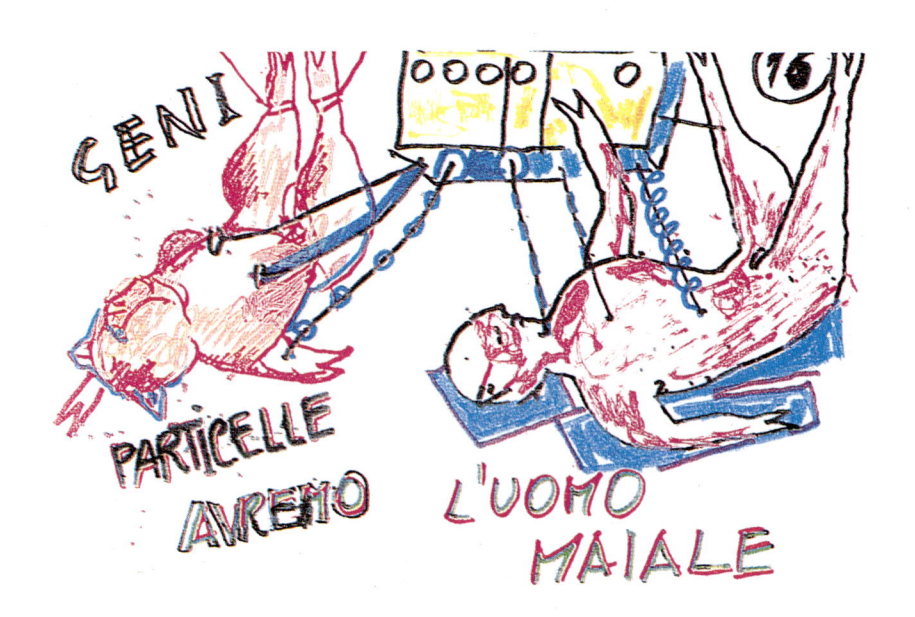

IMPORRE A OGNI PARTE
IL COPY-RIGHT
BREVETTARE
PAGARE I DIRITTI D'AUTORE
PER OGNI PEZZO
ALL'INDUSTRIA
PADRONA DEL BREVETTO

MALATTIE MORBI
E DEFORMAZIONI
OPTIONAL INCLUSI NEL PREZZO

STANNO SCHERZANDO
STORIA FARSESCA

INFORMARE 18
CRITICAMENTE
I GIOVANI
NON SANNO DELLE STRAGI
DI STATO
INCHIESTE DEVIATE
PROCESSI FARSA
DI STATO

CANTATE UOMINI LA VOSTRA STORIA

SAVINIO

CONTINUIAMO A CANTARE PER L'INDIGNAZIONE DEI GIOVANI

A COROLLARIO DI 20
QUESTA SERIE DI
SOPRAFFAZIONI
SOFRI
PIETROSTEFANI
BOMPRESSI
FARSA DI GIUSTIZIA
INSULTO ALLA RAGIONE

81

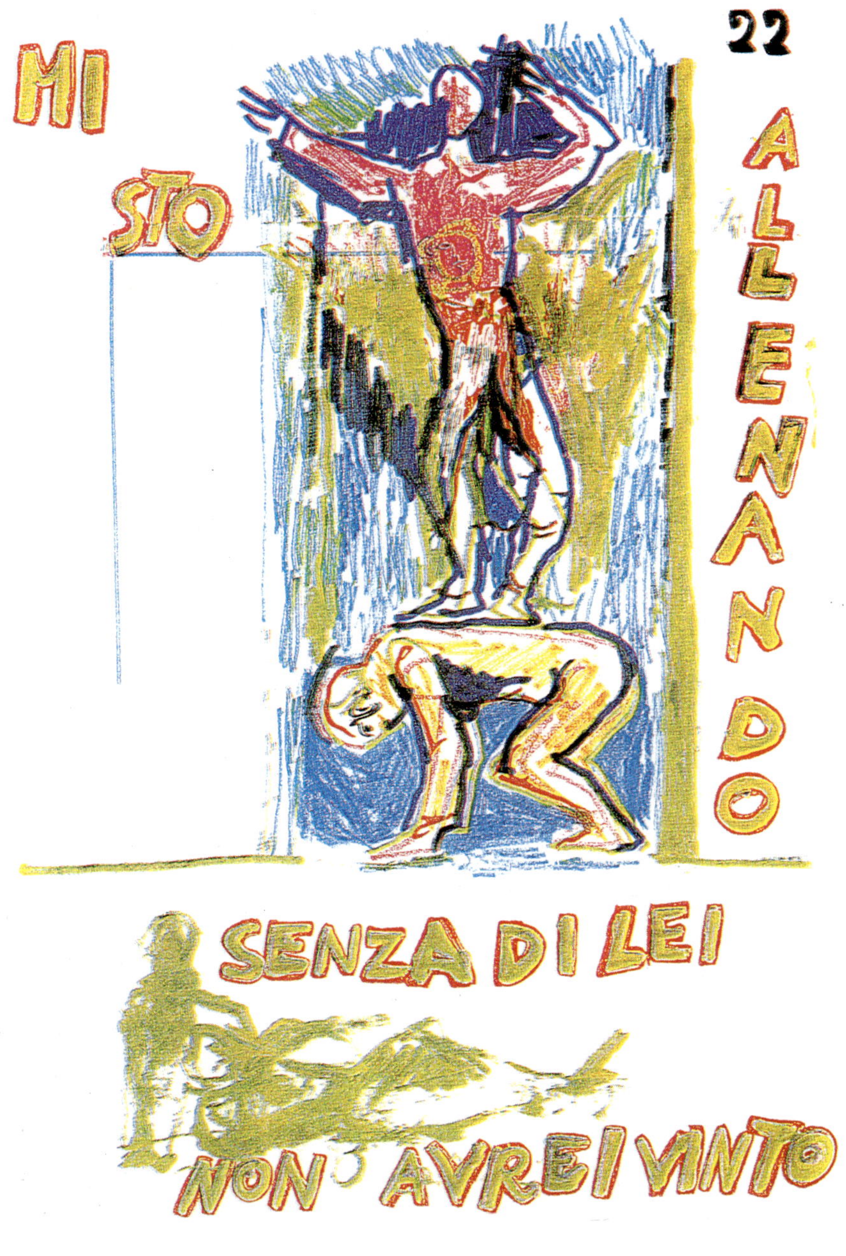
22
MI
STO
ALLENANDO
SENZA DI LEI
NON AVREI VINTO

## NELLE FABBRICHE OCCUPATE 23

## LA VIOLENZA SUBITA INSIEME

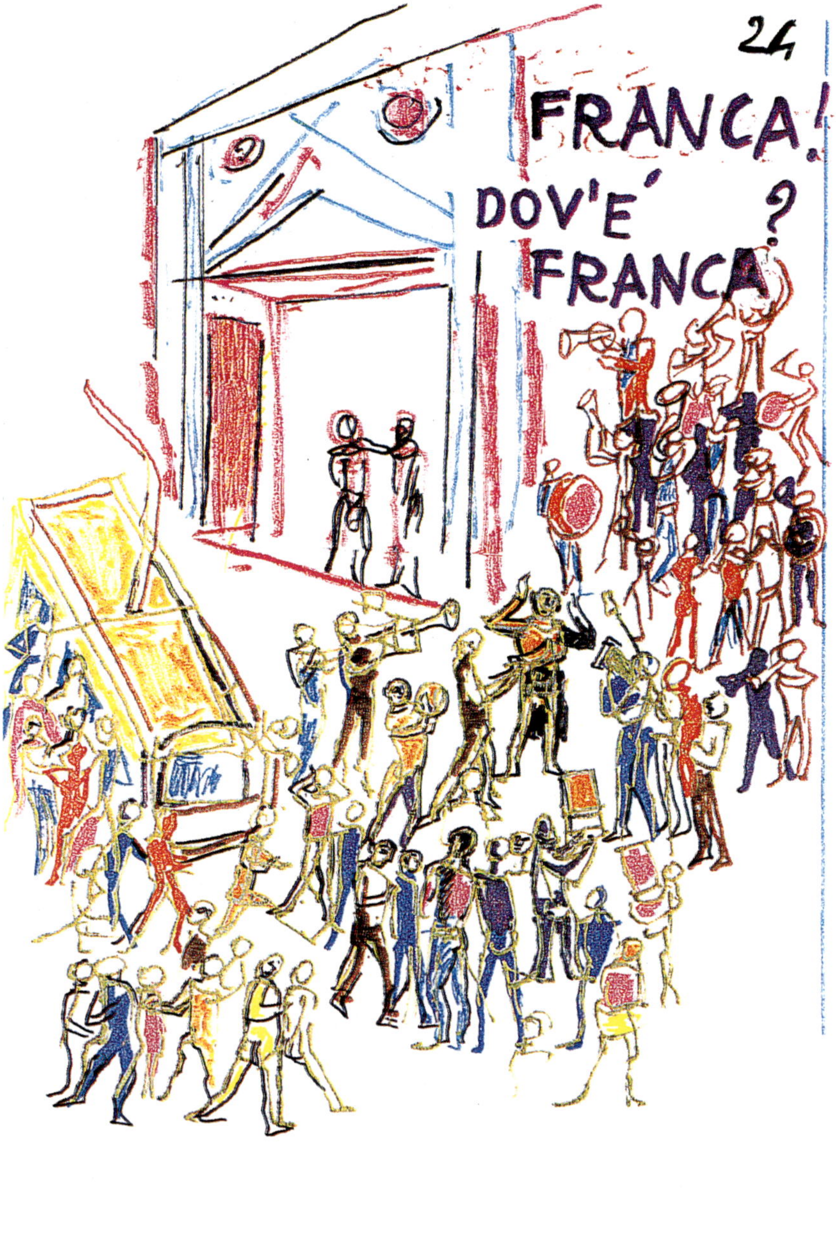
24
FRANCA!
DOV'E' FRANCA?

25

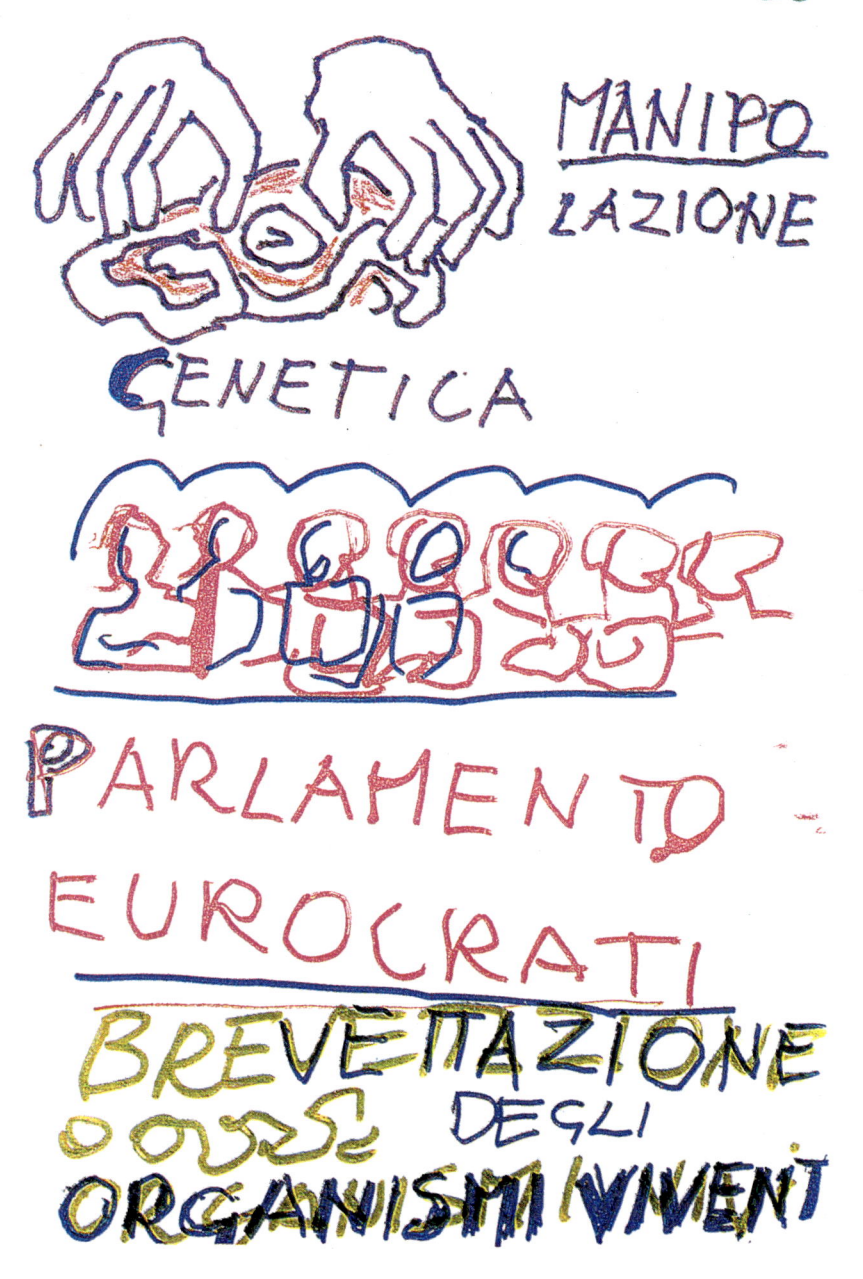

MANIPOLAZIONE GENETICA

PARLAMENTO EUROCRATI

BREVETTAZIONE DEGLI ORGANISMI VIVENT

Literature 1998

# JOSÉ SARAMAGO

*"who with parables sustained by imagination, compassion and irony enables us once again to apprehend an elusory reality"*

# THE NOBEL PRIZE IN LITERATURE

Speech by Professor Kjell Espmark of the Swedish Academy. Translation of the Swedish text.

Your Majesties, Your Royal Highness, Ladies and Gentlemen,

There is one type of writer who, like a bird of prey, circles time and again over the same territory. Book succeeds book, in progress towards a coherent picture of the world. José Saramago belongs to the opposite category, writers who repeatedly seem to want to invent both a world and a style that is new. In his novel *The Stone Raft* he makes the Iberian peninsula separate and drift out into the Atlantic, an opening that provides a wealth of possibilities for a satirical description of society. But in his next book, *The History of the Siege of Lisbon,* no trace of this geological catastrophe is to be found. In *Blindness,* a novel, the epidemic that deprives people of their sight is confined between the covers of the work. In his next novel, *All the Names,* at the Population Registration Office nothing has been heard of any rampant spread of blindness, nor in previous works has there been anything to suggest the existence of this chillingly all-embracing agency. It is not Saramago's ambition to portray a coherent universe. On the contrary, he seems every time to be trying out a new model to apprehend an evasive reality, fully aware that each model is a crude approximation that could permit other approximate values, indeed one that requires them. He explicitly condemns anything that claims to be "the only version"; it is merely "another version among many". There is no overriding truth. Saramago's apparently contradictory images of the world have to be placed alongside each other to provide their own alternative accounts of an existence that is fundamentally protean and unfathomable.

In each and everyone of these versions, the rules of common sense are suspended in some way. This is not uncommon in recent fiction. But here we are dealing with something different from narrative in which anything can happen — and does so all the time. Saramago has adopted a demanding artistic discipline which allows the laws of nature or common sense to be violated in one decisive respect only, and which then follows the consequences of this irrationality with all the logical rationality and exact observation it is capable of. In his novel *The Year of the Death of Ricardo Reis* he makes a flesh and blood character of a figure that has only existed in the imaginary world, one of the guises adopted by the poet Pessoa. But this miracle gives rise to a masterfully realistic picture of Lisbon in the 1930s. Again, the severance of the Iberian peninsula that allows it to drift off into the Atlantic is a one-off violation of the natural order; what follows is a hilariously precise description of the consequences of this absurd aberration. In *The History of the Siege of Lisbon* the accepted order of things is subverted more discreetly. A proof-reader introduces a "not" into a book about the war of liberation against the Moors, thus altering the course of history. As penance he is made to write an alternative history that delineates the consequences of his amendment; this is once again a version that denies any claim to be the only valid one. In the same spirit, Saramago has also published a new, wonderful version of the narrative of the gospels, a version in which the contravention of the expected order is to be found in God's petty hunger for power so that the role of Jesus is redefined as one of defiance. Perhaps the greatest scope allowed to the fantastic is in *Baltazar and Blimunda* where the clairvoyant heroine gathers up the wills of the dying — energy that makes the aerial voyage in the book possible. But she too and her love are placed in an objectively described historical process, in this case the construction of the convent at Mafra that cost so much human suffering.

This rich work, with its constantly shifting perspectives and constantly renewed images of the world, is held together by a narrator whose voice is with us all the time. Apparently he is a story-teller of the old-fashioned omniscient variety, a master of ceremonies standing on the stage next to his creations, commenting on them, guiding their steps and sometimes winking at us across the footlights. But Saramago uses these traditional techniques with amused distance. The narrator is also adept in the contemporary devices of the absurd and develops a modern scepticism when faced with the omniscient claim to be able to say how things stand. The result is literature characterised at one and the same time by sagacious reflection and by insight into the limitations of sagacity, by the fantastic and by precise realism, by cautious empathy and by critical acuity, by warmth and by irony. This is Saramago's unique amalgam.

Dear José Saramago,

Anybody who tries in a few minutes to portray your work will end up articulating a series of paradoxes. You have created a cosmos that does not want to be a coherent universe. You have given us ingenious versions of a history that will not allow itself to be taken captive. You have taken the stage as the kind of narrator we feel we have long been familiar with — but with all of our contemporary liberties at your fingertips and imbued with contemporary scepticism about definite knowledge. Your distinguishing mark is irony coupled with discerning empathy, distance without distance. It is my hope that this award will attract many people to your rich and complex world. I would like to express the warm congratulations of the Swedish Academy as I now request you to receive this year's Nobel Prize for Literature from the hands of His Majesty the King.

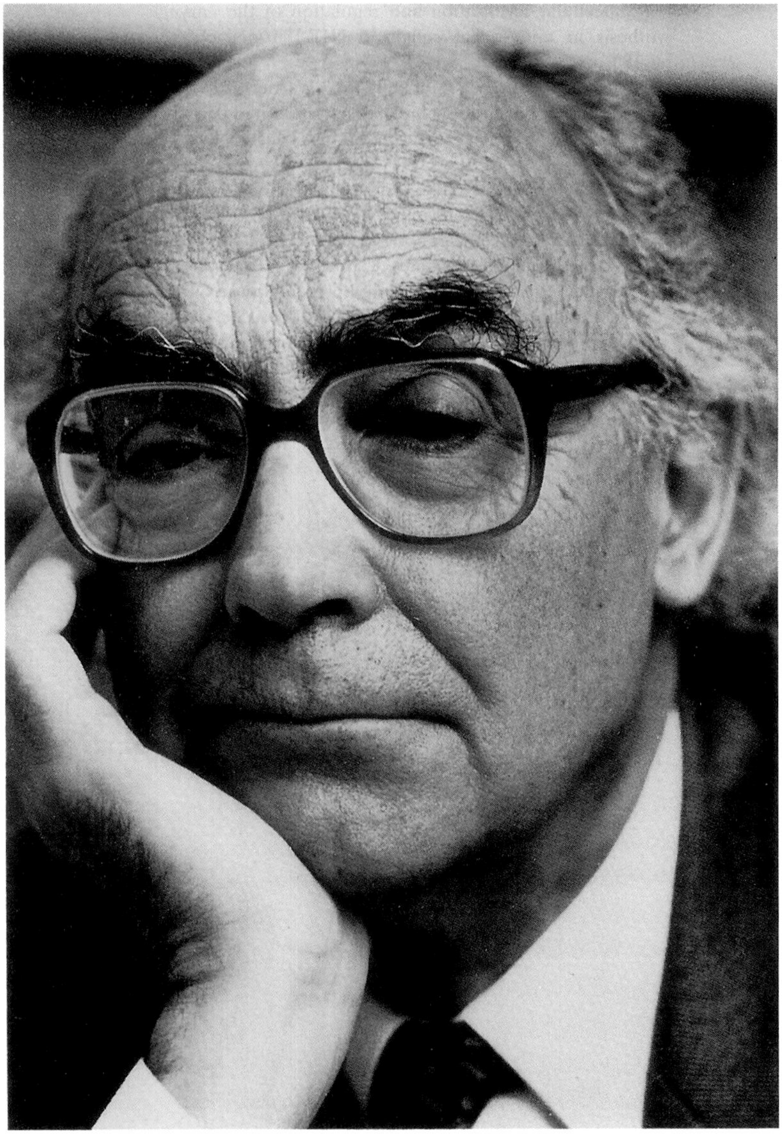

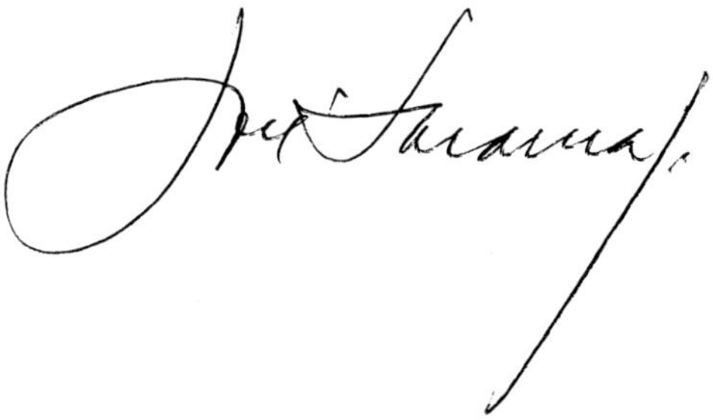

# JOSÉ SARAMAGO

*Written over the author's signature and translated into English by* Fernando Rodrigues *and* Tim Crosfield

I was born in a family of landless peasants, in Azinhaga, a small village in the province of Ribatejo, on the right bank of the Almonda River, around a hundred kilometres north-east of Lisbon. My parents were José de Sousa and Maria da Piedade. José de Sousa would have been my own name had not the Registrar, on his own initiative, added the nickname by which my father's family was known in the village: Saramago. I should add that *saramago* is a wild herbaceous plant, whose leaves in those times served at need as nourishment for the poor. Not until the age of seven, when I had to present an identification document at primary school, was it realised that my full name was José de Sousa Saramago...

This was not, however, the only identity problem to which I was fated at birth. Though I had come into the world on 16 November 1922, my official documents show that I was born two days later, on the 18th. It was thanks to this petty fraud that my family escaped from paying the fine for not having registered my birth at the proper legal time.

Maybe because he had served in World War I, in France as an artillery soldier, and had known other surroundings from those of the village, my father decided in 1924 to leave farm work and move with his family to Lisbon, where he started as a policeman, for which job were required no more "literary qualifications" (a common expression then...) than reading, writing and arithmetic.

A few months after settling in the capital my brother Francisco, who was two years older, died. Though our living conditions had improved a little after moving, we were never going to be well off.

I was already 13 or 14 when we moved, at last, to our own — but very tiny — house: till then we had lived in parts of houses, with other families. During all this time, and until I came of age, I spent many, and very often quite long, periods in the village with my mother's parents Jerónimo Meirinho and Josefa Caixinha.

I was a good pupil at primary school: in the second class I was writing with no spelling mistakes and the third and fourth classes were done in a single year. Then I was moved up to the grammar school where I stayed two years, with excellent marks in the first year, not so good in the second, but was well liked by classmates and teachers, even being elected (I was then 12...) treasurer of the Students' Union... Meanwhile my parents reached the conclusion that, in the absence of resources, they could not go on keeping me in the grammar school. The only alternative was to go to a technical school. And so it was: for five years I learned to be a mechanic. But surprisingly the syllabus at that time, though obviously technically oriented, included, besides French, a literature subject. As I had no books at home (my own books, bought by myself, however with money borrowed from a friend, I would only have when I was 19) the Portuguese language textbooks, with their "anthological" character, were what opened to me the doors of literary fruition: even today I can recite poetry learnt in that distant era. After finishing the course, I worked for two years as a mechanic at a car repair shop. By that time I had already started to frequent, in its evening opening hours, a public library in Lisbon. And it was there, with no help or guidance except curiosity and the will to learn, that my taste for reading developed and was refined.

When I got married in 1944, I had already changed jobs. I was now working in the Social Welfare Service as an administrative civil servant. My wife, Ilda Reis, then a typist with the Railway Company, was to become, many years later, one of the most important Portuguese engravers. She died in 1998. In 1947, the year of the birth of my only child, Violante, I published my first book, a novel I myself entitled *The Widow*, but which for editorial reasons appeared as *The Land of Sin*. I wrote another novel, *The Skylight*, still unpublished, and started another one, but did not get past the first few pages: its title was to be *Honey and Gall*, or maybe *Louis, son of Tadeus*... The matter was settled when I abandoned the project: it was becoming quite clear to me that I had nothing worthwhile to say. For 19 years, till 1966, when I got to publish *Possible Poems*, I was absent from the Portuguese literary scene, where few people can have noticed my absence.

For political reasons I became unemployed in 1949, but thanks to the goodwill of a former teacher at the technical school, I managed to find work at the metal company where he was a manager.

At the end of the 1950s I started working at a publishing company, Estúdios Cor, as production manager, so returning, but not as an author, to the world of letters I had left some years before. This new activity allowed me acquaintance and friendship with some of the most important Portuguese writers of the time. In 1955, to improve the family budget, but also because I enjoyed it, I started to spend part of my free time in translation, an activity that would continue till 1981: Colette, Pär Lagerkvist, Jean Cassou, Maupassant, André Bonnard, Tolstoy, Baudelaire, Étienne Balibar, Nikos Poulantzas, Henri Focillon, Jacques Roumain, Hegel, Raymond Bayer were some of the authors I translated. Between May 1967 and November 1968, I had another parallel occupation as a literary critic. Meanwhile, in 1966, I had published *Possible Poems*, a poetry book that marked my return to literature. After that, in 1970, another book of poems, *Probably Joy* and shortly after, in 1971 and 1973 respectively, under the titles *From this World and the Other* and *The Traveller's Baggage*, two collections of newspaper articles which the critics consider essential to the full understanding of my later work. After my divorce in 1970, I initiated a relationship, which would last till 1986, with the Portuguese writer Isabel da Nóbrega.

After leaving the publisher at the end of 1971, I worked for the following two years at the evening newspaper *Diário de Lisboa*, as manager of a cultural supplement and as an editor.

Published in 1974 with the title *The Opinions the DL Had*, those texts represent a very precise "reading" of the last time of the dictatorship, which was to be toppled that April. In April 1975, I became deputy director of the morning paper *Diário de Notícias*, a post I filled till that November and from which I was sacked in the aftermath of the changes provoked by the politico-military coup of the 25th November which blocked the revolutionary process. Two books mark this era: *The Year of 1993*, a long poem published in 1975, which some critics consider a herald of the works that two years later would start to appear with *Manual of Painting and Calligraphy*, a novel, and, under the title of *Notes*, the political articles I had published in the newspaper of which I had been a director.

Unemployed again and bearing in mind the political situation we were undergoing, without the faintest possibility of finding a job, I decided to devote myself to literature: it was about time to find out what I was worth as a writer. At the beginning of 1976,

I settled for some weeks in Lavre, a country village in Alentejo Province. It was that period of study, observation and note-taking that led, in 1980, to the novel *Risen from the Ground*, where the way of narrating which characterises my novels was born. Meanwhile, in 1978 I had published a collection of short stories, *Quasi Object;* in 1979 the play *The Night*, and after that, a few months before *Risen from the Ground*, a new play, *What shall I do with this Book?*. With the exception of another play, entitled *The Second Life of Francis of Assisi*, published in 1987, the 1980s were entirely dedicated to the Novel: *Baltazar and Blimunda*, 1982, *The Year of the Death of Ricardo Reis*, 1984, *The Stone Raft*, 1986, *The History of the Siege of Lisbon*, 1989. In 1986, I met the Spanish journalist Pilar del Río. We got married in 1988.

In consequence of the Portuguese government censorship of *The Gospel According to Jesus Christ* (1991), vetoing its presentation for the European Literary Prize under the pretext that the book was offensive to Catholics, my wife and I transferred our residence to the island of Lanzarote in the Canaries. At the beginning of that year I published the play *In Nomine Dei*, which had been written in Lisbon, from which the libretto for the opera *Divara* would be taken, with music by the Italian composer Azio Corghi and staged for the first time in Münster, Germany in 1993. This was not the first cooperation with Corghi: his also is the music to the opera *Blimunda*, from my novel *Baltazar and Blimunda*, staged in Milan, Italy in 1990. In 1993, I started writing a diary, *Cadernos de Lanzarote* (Lanzarote Diaries), with five volumes so far. In 1995, I published the novel *Blindness* and in 1997 *All the Names*. In 1995, I was awarded the Camões Prize and in 1998 the Nobel Prize for Literature.

In 2000, José Saramago published the novel *A caverna* (The Cavern).

# HOW CHARACTERS BECAME THE MASTERS AND THE AUTHOR THEIR APPRENTICE

Nobel Lecture, December 7, 1998
by
JOSÉ SARAMAGO
Tiás, Lanzarote, Spain

The wisest man I ever knew in my whole life could not read or write. At four o'clock in the morning, when the promise of a new day still lingered overFrench lands, he got up from his pallet and left for the fields, taking to pasture the half-dozen pigs whose fertility nourished him and his wife. My mother's parents lived on this scarcity, on the small breeding of pigs that after weaning were sold to the neighbours in our village of Azinhaga in the province of Ribatejo. Their names were Jerónimo Meirinho and Josefa Caixinha and they were both illiterate. In winter when the cold of the night grew to the point of freezing the water in the pots inside the house, they went to the sty and fetched the weaklings among the piglets, taking them to their bed. Under the coarse blankets, the warmth from the humans saved the little animals from freezing and rescued them from certain death. Although the two were kindly people, it was not a compassionate soul that prompted them to act in that way: what concerned them, without sentimentalism or rhetoric, was to protect their daily bread, as is natural for people who, to maintain their life, have not learnt to think more than is needful. Many times I helped my grandfather Jerónimo in his swineherd's labour, many times I dug the land in the vegetable garden adjoining the house, and I chopped wood for the fire, many times, turning and turning the big iron wheel which worked the water pump. I pumped water from the community well and carried it on my shoulders. Many times, in secret, dodging from the men guarding the cornfields, I went with my grandmother, also at dawn, armed with rakes, sacking and cord, to glean the stubble, the loose straw that would then serve as litter for the livestock. And sometimes, on hot summer nights, after supper, my grandfather would tell me: "José, tonight we're going to sleep, both of us, under the fig tree". There were two other fig trees, but that one, certainly because it was the biggest, because it was the oldest, and timeless, was, for everybody in the house, the fig tree. More or less by antonomasia, an erudite word that I met only many years after and learned the meaning of... Amongst the peace of the night, amongst the tree's high branches a star appeared to me and then slowly hid behind a leaf while, turning my gaze in another direction, I saw rising into view like a river flowing silent through the hollow sky, the opal clarity of the Milky Way, the Road to Santiago as we still used to call it in the village. With sleep delayed, night was peopled with the stories and the cases my grandfather told and told: legends, apparitions, terrors, unique episodes, old deaths, scuffles with sticks and stones, the words of our forefathers, an untiring rumour of memories that would keep me awake while at the same time gently lulling me. I could never know if he was silent when he realised that I had fallen asleep or if he kept on talking so as not to leave half-unanswered the question I invariably asked into the most delayed pauses he placed on purpose within the account: "And what happened next?" Maybe he repeated the stories for himself, so as not to forget them, or else to enrich them with new detail. At that age and as we all do at some time, needless to say, I imagined my grandfather Jerónimo was master of all the knowledge in the world. When at first light the singing of birds woke me up, he was not there any longer, had gone to the field with his animals, letting me sleep on. Then I would get up, fold the coarse blanket and barefoot — in the village I always walked barefoot till I was fourteen — and with straws still stuck in my hair, I went from the cultivated part of the yard to the other part, where the sties were, by the house. My grandmother, already afoot before my grandfather, set in front of me a big bowl of coffee with pieces of bread in and asked me if I had slept well. If I told her some bad dream, born of my grandfather's stories, she always reassured me: "Don't make much of it, in dreams there's nothing solid". At the time I thought, though my grandmother was also a very wise woman, she couldn't rise to the heights grandfather could, a man who, lying under a fig tree, having at his side José his grandson, could set the universe in motion just with a couple of words. It was only many years after, when my grandfather had departed from this world and I was a grown man, I finally came to realise that my grandmother, after all, also believed in dreams. There could have been no other reason why, sitting one evening at the door of her cottage where she now lived alone, staring at the biggest and smallest stars overhead, she said these words: "The world is so beautiful and it is such a pity that I have to die". She didn't say she was afraid of dying, but that it was a pity to die, as if her hard life of unrelenting work was, in that almost final moment, receiving the grace of a supreme and last farewell, the consolation of beauty revealed. She was sitting at the door of a house like none other I can imagine in all the world, because in it lived people who could sleep with piglets as if they were their own children, people who were sorry to leave life just because the world was beautiful; and this Jerónimo, my grandfather, swineherd and story-teller, feeling death about to arrive and take him, went and said goodbye to the trees in the yard, one by one, embracing them and crying because he knew he wouldn't see them again.

Many years later, writing for the first time about my grandfather Jerónimo and my grandmother Josefa (I haven't said so far that she was, according to many who knew her when young, a woman of uncommon beauty), I was finally aware I was transforming the ordinary people they were into literary characters: this was, probably, my way of not forgetting them, drawing and redrawing their faces with the pencil that ever changes memory, colouring and illuminating the monotony of a dull and horizonless daily routine as if creating, over the unstable map of memory, the supernatural unreality of the country where one has decided to spend one's life. The same attitude of mind that, after evoking the fascinating and enigmatic figure of a certain Berber grandfather, would lead me to describe more or less in these words an old photo (now almost eighty years old) showing my parents "both standing, beautiful and young, facing the photographer, showing in their faces an expression of solemn seriousness, maybe fright in front of the camera at the very instant when the lens is about to capture the image they will never have again, because the following day will be, implacably, another day... My mother is leaning her right elbow against a tall pillar and holds, in her right hand drawn in to her body, a flower. My father has his arm round my mother's back, his callused hand showing over her shoulder, like a wing. They are standing, shy, on a carpet patterned with branches. The canvas forming the fake background of the picture shows diffuse and incongruous neo-classic architecture." And I ended, "The day will come when I will tell these things. Nothing of this matters except to me. A Berber grandfather from North Africa, another grandfather a swineherd, a wonderfully beautiful grandmother; serious and handsome parents, a flower in a picture — what other genealogy would I care for? and what better tree would I lean against?"

I wrote these words almost thirty years ago, having no other purpose than to rebuild and register instants of the lives of those people who engendered and were closest to my being, thinking that nothing else would need explaining for people to know where I came from and what materials the person I am was made of, and what I have become little by little. But after all I was wrong, biology doesn't determine everything and as for genetics, very mysterious must have been its paths to make its voyages so long... My genealogical tree (you will forgive the presumption of naming it this way, being so diminished in the substance of its sap) lacked not only some of those branches that time and life's successive encounters cause to burst from the main stem but also someone to help its roots penetrate the deepest subterranean layers, someone who could verify the consistency and flavour of its fruit, someone to extend and strengthen its top to make of it a shelter for birds of passage and a support for nests. When painting my parents and grandparents with the paints of literature, transforming them from common people of flesh and blood into characters, newly and in different ways builders of my life, I was, without noticing, tracing the path by which the characters I would invent later on, the others, truly literary, would construct and bring to me the materials and the tools which, at last, for better or for worse, in the sufficient and in the insufficient, in profit and loss, in all that is scarce but also in what is too much, would make of me the person whom I nowadays recognise as myself: the creator of those characters but at the same time their own creation. In one sense it could even be said that, letter-by-letter, word-by-word, page-by-page, book after book, I have been successively implanting in the man I was the characters I created. I believe that without them I wouldn't be the person I am today; without them maybe my life wouldn't have succeeded in becoming more than an inexact sketch, a promise that like so many others remained only a promise, the existence of someone who maybe might have been but in the end could not manage to be.

Now I can clearly see those who were my life-masters, those who most intensively taught me the hard work of living, those dozens of characters from my novels and plays that right now I see marching past before my eyes, those men and women of paper and ink, those people I believed I was guiding as I the narrator chose according to my whim, obedient to my will as an author, like articulated puppets whose actions could have no more effect on me than the burden and the tension of the strings I moved them with. Of those masters, the first was, undoubtedly, a mediocre portrait-painter, whom I called simply H, the main character of a story that I feel may reasonably be called a double initiation (his own, but also in a manner of speaking the author's) entitled *Manual of Painting and Calligraphy*, who taught me the simple honesty of acknowledging and observing, without resentment or frustration, my own limitations: as I could not and did not aspire to venture beyond my little plot of cultivated land, all I had left was the possibility of digging down, underneath, towards the roots. My own but also the world's, if I can be allowed such an immoderate ambition. It's not up to me, of course, to evaluate the merits of the results of efforts made, but today I consider it obvious that all my work from then on has obeyed that purpose and that principle.

Then came the men and women of Alentejo, that same brotherhood of the condemned of the earth where belonged my grandfather Jerónimo and my grandmother Josefa, primitive peasants obliged to hire out the strength of their arms for a wage and working conditions that deserved only to be called infamous, getting for less than nothing a life which the cultivated and civilised beings we are proud to be are pleased to call — depending on the occasion — precious, sacred or sublime. Common people I knew, deceived by a Church both accomplice and beneficiary of the power of the State and of the landlords, people permanently watched by the police, people so many times innocent victims of the arbitrariness of a false justice. Three generations of a peasant family, the Badweathers, from the beginning of the century to the April Revolution of 1974 which toppled dictatorship, move through this novel, called *Risen from the Ground*, and it was with such men and women risen from the ground, real people first, figures of fiction later, that I learned how to be patient, to trust and to confide in time, that same time that simultaneously builds and destroys us in order to build and once more to destroy us. The only thing I am not sure of having assimilated satisfactorily is something that the hardship of those experiences turned into virtues in those women and men: a naturally austere attitude towards life. Having in mind, however, that the lesson learned still after more than twenty years remains intact in my memory, that every day I feel its presence in my spirit like a persistent summons: I haven't lost, not yet at least, the hope of meriting a little more the greatness of those examples of dignity proposed to me in the vast immensity of the plains of Alentejo. Time will tell.

What other lessons could I possibly receive from a Portuguese who lived in the sixteenth century, who composed the *Rimas* and the glories, the shipwrecks and the national disenchantments in the *Lusíadas*, who was an absolute poetical genius, the greatest in our literature, no matter how much sorrow this causes to Fernando Pessoa, who proclaimed himself its Super Camões? No lesson would fit me, no lesson could I learn, except the simplest, which could have been offered to me by Luís Vaz de Camões in his pure humanity, for instance the proud humility of an author who goes knocking at every door looking for someone willing to publish the book he has written, thereby suffering the scorn of the ignoramuses of blood and race, the disdainful indifference of a king and of his powerful entourage, the mockery with which the world has always received the visits of poets, visionaries and fools. At least once in life, every author has been, or will have to be, Luís de Camões, even if they haven't written the poem *Sôbolos Rios...* Among nobles, courtiers and censors from the Holy Inquisition, among the loves of yester-year and the disillusionments of premature old age, between the pain of writing and the joy of having written, it was this ill man, returning poor from India where so many sailed just to get rich, it was this soldier blind in one eye, slashed in his soul, it was this seducer of no fortune who will never again flutter the hearts of the ladies in the royal court, whom I put on stage in a play called *What shall I do with this Book?*, whose ending repeats another question, the only truly important one, the one we will never know if it will ever have a sufficient answer: "What will you do with this book?". It was also proud humility to carry under his arm a masterpiece and to be unfairly rejected by the world. Proud humility also, and obstinate too — wanting to know what the purpose will be, tomorrow, of the books we are writing today, and immediately doubting whether they will last a long time (how long?) the reassuring reasons we are given or that are given us by ourselves. No-one is better deceived than when he allows others to deceive him.

Here comes a man whose left hand was taken in war and a woman who came to this world with the mysterious power of seeing what lies beyond people's skin. His name is Baltazar Mateus and his nickname Seven-Suns; she is known as Blimunda and also, later, as Seven-Moons because it is written that where there is a sun there will have to be a moon and that only the conjoined and harmonious presence of the one and the other will, through love, make earth habitable. There also approaches a Jesuit priest called Bartolomeu who invented a machine capable of going up to the sky and flying with no other fuel than the human will, the will which, people say, can do anything, the will that could not, or did not know how to, or until today did not want to, be the sun and the moon of simple kindness or of even simpler respect. These three Portuguese fools from the eighteenth century, in a time and country where superstition and the fires of the Inquisition flourished, where vanity and the megalomania of a king raised a convent, a palace and a basilica which would amaze the outside world, if that world, in a very unlikely supposition, had eyes enough to see Portugal, eyes like Blimunda's, eyes to see what was hidden... Here also comes a crowd of thousands and thousands of men with dirty and callused hands, exhausted bodies after having lifted year after year, stone-by-stone, the implacable convent walls, the huge palace rooms, the columns and pilasters, the airy belfries, the basilica dome suspended over empty space. The sounds we hear are from Domenico Scarlatti's harpsichord, and he doesn't quite know if he is supposed to be laughing or crying... This is the story of *Baltazar and Blimunda*, a book where the apprentice author, thanks to what had long ago been taught to him in his grandparents' Jerónimo's and Josefa's time, managed to write some similar words not without poetry: "Besides women's talk, dreams are what hold the world in its orbit. But it is also dreams that crown it with moons, that's why the sky is the splendour in men's heads, unless men's heads are the one and only sky." So be it.

Of poetry the teenager already knew some lessons, learnt in his textbooks when, in a technical school in Lisbon, he was being prepared for the trade he would have at the beginning of his labour's life: mechanic. He also had good poetry masters during long evening hours in public libraries, reading at random, with finds from catalogues, with no guidance, no-one to advise him, with the creative amazement of the sailor who invents every place he discovers. But it was at the Industrial School Library that *The Year of the Death of Ricardo Reis* started to be written... There, one day the young mechanic (he was about seventeen) found a magazine entitled *Atena* containing poems signed with that name and, naturally, being very poorly acquainted with the literary cartography of his country, he thought that there really was a Portuguese poet called Ricardo Reis. Very soon, though, he found that this poet was really one Fernando Nogueira Pessoa, who signed his works with the names of non-existent poets, born of his mind. He called them heteronyms, a word that did not exist in the dictionaries of the time which is why it was so hard for the apprentice to letters to know what it meant. He learnt many of Ricardo Reis' poems by heart ("To be great, be one/ Put yourself into the little things you do"); but in spite of being so young and ignorant, he could not accept that a superior mind could really have conceived, without remorse, the cruel line "Wise is he who is satisfied with the spectacle of the world". Later, much later, the apprentice, already with grey hairs and a little wiser in his own wisdom, dared to write a novel to show this poet of the *Odes* something about the spectacle of the world of 1936, where he had placed him to live out his last few days: the occupation of the Rhineland by the Nazi army, Franco's war against the Spanish Republic, the creation by Salazar of the Portuguese Fascist militias. It was his way of telling him: "Here is the spectacle of the world, my poet of serene bitterness and elegant scepticism. Enjoy, behold, since to be sitting is your wisdom..."

*The Year of the Death of Ricardo Reis* ended with the melancholy words: "Here, where the sea has ended and land awaits." So there would be no more discoveries by Portugal, fated to one infinite wait for futures not even imaginable; only the usual fado, the same old saudade and little more... Then the apprentice imagined that there still might be a way of sending the ships back to the water, for instance, by moving the land and setting that out to sea. An immediate fruit of collective Portuguese resentment of the historical disdain of Europe (more accurate to say fruit of my own resentment...) the novel I then wrote — *The Stone Raft* — separated from the Continent the whole Iberian Peninsula and transformed it into a big floating island, moving of its own accord with no oars, no sails, no propellers, in a southerly direction, "a mass of stone and land, covered with cities, villages, rivers, woods, factories and bushes, arable land, with its people and animals" on its way to a new Utopia: the cultural meeting of the Peninsular peoples with the peoples from the other side of the Atlantic, thereby defying — my strategy went that far — the suffocating rule exercised over that region by the United States of America... A vision twice Utopian would see this political fiction as a much more generous and human metaphor: that Europe, all of it, should move South to help balance the world, as compensation for its former and its present colonial abuses. That is, Europe at last as an ethical reference. The characters in *The Stone Raft* — two women, three men and a dog — continually travel through the Peninsula as it furrows the ocean. The world is changing and they know they have to find in themselves the new persons they will become (not to mention the dog, he is not like other dogs...). This will suffice for them.

Then the apprentice recalled that at a remote time of his life he had worked as a proof-reader and that if, so to say, in *The Stone Raft* he had revised the future, now it might not be a bad thing to revise the past, inventing a novel to be called *History of the Siege of Lisbon*, where a proof-reader, checking a book with the same title but a real history book and tired of watching how "History" is less and less able to surprise, decides to substitute a "no" for a "yes", subverting the authority of "historical truth". Raimundo Silva, the proof-reader, is a simple, common man, distinguished from the crowd only by believing that all things have their visible sides and their invisible ones and that we will know nothing about them until we manage to see both. He talks about this with the historian thus: "I must remind you that proof-readers are serious people, much experienced in literature and life, My book, don't forget, deals with history. However, since I have no intention of pointing out other contradictions, in my modest opinion, Sir, everything that is not literature is life, History as well, Especially history, without wishing to give offence, And painting and music, Music has resisted since birth, it comes and goes, tries to free itself from the word, I suppose out of envy, only to submit in the end, And painting, Well now, painting is nothing more than literature achieved with paintbrushes, I trust you haven't forgotten that mankind began to paint long before it knew how to write, Are you familiar with the proverb, If you don't have a dog, go hunting with a cat, in other words, the man who cannot write, paints or draws, as if he were a child, What you are trying to say, in other words, is that literature already existed before it was born, Yes, Sir, just like man who, in a manner of speaking, existed before he came into being, It strikes me that you have missed your vocation, you should have become a philosopher, or historian, you have the flair and temperament needed for these disciplines, I lack the necessary training, Sir, and what can a simple man achieve without training, I was more than fortunate to come into the world with my genes in order, but in a raw state as it were, and then no education beyond primary school, You could have presented yourself as being self-taught, the product of your own worthy efforts, there's nothing to be ashamed of, society in the past took pride in its autodidacts, No longer, progress has come along and put an end to all of that, now the self-taught are frowned upon, only those who write entertaining verses and stories are entitled to be and go on being autodidacts, lucky for them, but as for me, I must confess that I never had any talent for literary creation, Become a philosopher, man, You have a keen sense of humour, Sir, with a distinct flair for irony, and I ask myself how you ever came to devote yourself to history, serious and profound science as it is, I'm only ironic in real life, It has always struck me that history is not real life, literature, yes, and nothing else, But history was real life at the time when it could not yet be called history, So you believe, Sir, that history is real life, Of course, I do, I meant to say that history was real life, No doubt at all, What would become of us if the deleatur did not exist, sighed the proof-reader." It is useless to add that the apprentice had learnt, with Raimundo Silva, the lesson of doubt. It was about time.

Well, probably it was this learning of doubt that made him go through the writing of *The Gospel According to Jesus Christ*. True, and he has said so, the title was the result of an optical illusion, but it is fair to ask whether it was the serene example of the proof-reader who, all the time, had been preparing the ground from where the new novel would gush out. This time it was not a matter of looking behind the pages of the New Testament searching for antitheses, but of illuminating their surfaces, like that of a painting, with a low light to heighten their relief, the traces of crossings, the shadows of depressions. That's how the apprentice read, now surrounded by evangelical characters, as if for the first time, the description of the massacre of the innocents and, having read, he couldn't understand.

He couldn't understand why there were already martyrs in a religion that would have to wait thirty years more to listen to its founder pronouncing the first word about it, he could not understand why the only person that could have done so dared not save the lives of the children of Bethlehem, he could not understand Joseph's lack of a minimum feeling of responsibility, of remorse, of guilt, or even of curiosity, after returning with his family from Egypt. It cannot even be argued in defence that it was necessary for the children of Bethlehem to die to save the life of Jesus: simple common sense, that should preside over all things human and divine, is there to remind us that God would not send His Son to Earth, particularly with the mission of redeeming the sins of mankind, to die beheaded by a soldier of Herod at the age of two... In that Gospel, written by the apprentice with the great respect due to great drama, Joseph will be aware of his guilt, will accept remorse as a punishment for the sin he has committed and will be taken to die almost without resistance, as if this were the last remaining thing to do to clear his accounts with the world. The apprentice's Gospel is not, consequently, one more edifying legend of blessed beings and gods, but the story of a few human beings subjected to a power they fight but cannot defeat. Jesus, who will inherit the dusty sandals with which his father had walked so many country roads, will also inherit his tragic feeling of responsibility and guilt that will never abandon him, not even when he raises his voice from the top of the cross: "Men, forgive him because he knows not what he has done", referring certainly to the God who has sent him there, but perhaps also, if in that last agony he still remembers, his real father who has generated him humanly in flesh and blood. As you can see, the apprentice had already made a long voyage when in his heretical Gospel he wrote the last words of the temple dialogue between Jesus and the scribe: "Guilt is a wolf that eats its cub after having devoured its father, The wolf of which you speak has already devoured my father, Then it will be soon your turn, And what about you, have you ever been devoured, Not only devoured, but also spewed up".

Had Emperor Charlemagne not established a monastery in North Germany, had that monastery not been the origin of the city of Münster, had Münster not wished to celebrate its twelve-hundredth anniversary with an opera about the dreadful sixteenth-century war between Protestant Anabaptists and Catholics, the apprentice would not have written his play *In Nomine Dei*. Once more, with no other help than the tiny light of his reason, the apprentice had to penetrate the obscure labyrinth of religious beliefs, the beliefs that so easily make human beings kill and be killed. And what he saw was, once again, the hideous mask of intolerance, an intolerance that in Münster became an insane paroxysm, an intolerance that insulted the very cause that, both parties claimed to defend. Because it was not a question of war in the name of two inimical gods, but of war in the name of a same god. Blinded by their own beliefs, the Anabaptists and the Catholics of Münster were incapable of understanding the most evident of all proofs: on Judgement Day, when both parties come forward to receive the reward or the punishment they deserve for their actions on earth, God — if His decisions are ruled by anything like human logic — will have to accept them all in Paradise, for the simple reason that they all believe in it. The terrible slaughter in Münster taught the apprentice that religions, despite all they promised, have never been used to bring men together and that the most absurd of all wars is a holy war, considering that God cannot, even if he wanted to, declare war on himself...

Blind. The apprentice thought, "we are blind", and he sat down and wrote *Blindness* to remind those who might read it that we pervert reason when we humiliate life, that human dignity is insulted every day by the powerful of our world, that the universal lie has replaced the plural truths, that man stopped respecting himself when he lost the respect due to his fellow-creatures. Then the apprentice, as if trying to exorcise the monsters generated by the blindness of reason, started writing the simplest of all stories: one person is looking for another, because he has realised that life has nothing more important to demand from a human being. The book is called *All the Names*. Unwritten, all our names are there. The names of the living and the names of the dead.

I conclude, The voice that read these pages wished to be the echo of the conjoined voices of my characters. I don't have, as it were, more voice than the voices they had. Forgive me if what has seemed little to you, to me is all.

*Translated from the Portuguese: Tim Crosfield and Fernando Rodrigues*

Literature 1999

# GÜNTER GRASS

*"whose frolicsome black fables portray the forgotten face of history"*

# THE NOBEL PRIZE IN LITERATURE

Speech by Dr. Horace Engdahl of the Swedish Academy.
Translation of the Swedish text.

Your Majesties, Your Royal Highness, Ladies and Gentlemen,

These days, we often hear talk of the diminishing importance of literature. We are told that it has been reduced to entertainment or to a hobby for an isolated elite. But just as a philosopher in ancient Greece, wishing to reject the Eleatic theory that motion is impossible, simply walked about in front of the Eleatics' meeting place in the hall of pillars, so having Günter Grass present is enough to make us realize that literature will not easily be pushed to the margin.

Publication of *The Tin Drum* meant a second birth for the German novel of the twentieth century. Not since Thomas Mann's *Buddenbrooks* had a first book caused such a stir. This kind of attention has its price. Just like Mann, Grass later met with the reproach that, after being so loved by readers and critics, he had the audacity to write ... differently. In Thomas Mann's case, this reproach turned up even in the Swedish Academy's citation for his Nobel Prize in 1929. The 1999 citation contains no such reservation.

To the merits of Günter Grass belong not only his creation of a narrative carnival like *The Tin Drum*, but also the fact that he hasn't spent his life trying to repeat this feat. Time and again, he has left behind the established critical measures of his greatness and ventured with astonishing liberty into new undertakings. He has set himself above prohibitions and expectations, esthetical as well as political. He continues to do so in the newest texts that have come from his workshop.

It's often said that, with *The Tin Drum*, Grass saved a vanished world from oblivion — the town of Danzig as it existed before the Nazis and the war. But readers intent on a magical time tour should perhaps rather read *Cat and Mouse*, the short story in which the friendships of boyhood are recalled with the keenness of loss and guilt. *The Tin Drum*, however, is something else. It seems to stage the very march of history with a formidable array of characters and tall stories. But everything is viewed from an unusually low position a yard above the ground. *The Tin Drum* has its temper from a first person narrator who resembles nothing in literature or on earth. Regardless of all the tricksters of folklore, regardless of mythical infants equipped with the wisdom of old men, regardless of Shakespeare's Puck and Hoffmann's Kleinzach, Oskar Matzerath is a completely original creation: an infernal intelligence in the body of a three-year old, a monster who victoriously approaches mankind with the aid of a tin drum, an intellectual with infantility as his critical method. If, as one voice in the novel suggests, our time could wear the motto "Mysticism, barbarism, gloom," then Oskar is its sworn enemy. From Dadaism and other cheerfully destructive avant-garde groups of the beginning of our century, he has inherited the creative irreverence, but, unlike them, hasn't jettisoned reason.

Other German writers — I'm thinking of Arno Schmidt and Heinrich Böll — portrayed the collapse of human values as apocalypse or tragedy. Grass preferred a literary method more akin to the one adopted by the anonymous parodist who, some time after Homer, depicted martial heroism as the battle between the frogs and the mice. Grass broke the spell that lay over the German past and sabotaged the German sublime, the taste for the somberly blazing magnificence of foredoomed destruction. This was an achievement far more radical than all the ideological criticism directed against Nazism. Grass's novels strip their characters of grand words and emphasize the solidity of the flesh by bringing human forms close to the animal world. We all have a place in his menagerie of cat and mouse, dog, snail, flounder, frog and scarecrow.

The different books that followed — the feverish *Dog Years*, the patiently arguing diary novels from the period when the author was engaged in party politics, the great fables of the seventies and eighties and so on — taught us to read in a new way, with our ears and stomachs just as much as with our eyes and brains. Günter Grass in his expansive phrases brings together not only the high and the low but also the subject and its distorted representation in general opinion, that spiteful mutter for which no one is responsible and of which no one is innocent. His text displays not the homophony of letters but the polyphony of orality, like a noisy inn where a voice is raised without necessarily silencing friends and opponents. His irony has as many shades as his graphic prints.

The major codes of his work — animals and food — meet in *The Flounder*, a great novel of the formation and malformation of civilization. The author musters the courage to engage in a dialogue with feminism, and attempts a new version of the history of progress, here told as the story of how eminent female cooks taught the people to feed on appetizing and wholesome dishes. With the serious motto that you mustn't cook without historical consciousness, Grass develops a mode of thinking one would like to call *gastrosophy*.

In his much-debated *Ein Writes Feld* — *A Far Field* — Grass takes the daring step of giving an undramatic view of the relationship between the henchmen of totalitarianism and its victims. He plays off the eternal humanist against the eternal police informer, sympathetic understanding against the endless inquisition that keeps prying into old mistakes even beyond the grave. Of the two main characters he says: "Seen from the front, they looked very ill-matched, from behind however, as fitting to each other as two pieces of a jigsaw puzzle." There is something so hilariously insolent, independent and relativistic in Grass's rendering of life in Berlin around the Fall of the Wall, that he was bound to infuriate many readers of his home country.


Günter Grass,
Your sense of proportion has done mankind a genuine service. Your new book has the title *Mein Jahrhundert* — My Century. The fact that you are receiving the twentieth century's last Nobel Literature Prize is confirmation of the reasonableness of such a title. In your cavalcade of the past hundred years, you give ample proof of your uncanny ability to impersonate the voices of the thoughtless: all those bewitched by the hopes of politics and technology, rendered stupid by the great perspectives. The core of thoughtlessness is enthusiasm. I read *Mein Jahrhundert* as a critique of enthusiasm and a celebration of its opposite, a good memory. Your style, with its repetitions and specifications and stratification of different voices, tells us that we shall not be in a hurry either when dealing with the past or when dealing with the future. You have shown that as long as literature remembers what people hasten to forget, it remains a power to be reckoned with. I would like to express the warm congratulations of the Swedish Academy as I now request you to receive the Nobel Prize for Literature from the hands of His Majesty the King.

Photography by Hans Grunert

# GÜNTER GRASS

Günter Grass was born in 1927 in Danzig-Langfuhr of Polish-German parents. After military service and captivity by American forces 1944–46, he worked as a farm labourer and miner and studied art in Düsseldorf and Berlin. 1956–59 he made his living as a sculptor, graphic artist and writer in Paris, and subsequently Berlin. In 1955 Grass became a member of the socially critical Gruppe 47 (later described with great warmth in *The Meeting at Telgte*), his first poetry was published in 1956 and his first play produced in 1957. His major international breakthrough came in 1959 with his allegorical and wide-ranging picaresque novel *The Tin Drum* (filmed by Schlöndorff), a satirical panorama of German reality during the first half of this century, which, with *Cat and Mouse* and *Dog Years*, was to form what is called the Danzig Trilogy.

In the 1960s Grass became active in politics, participating in election campaigns on behalf of the Social Democrat party and Willy Brandt. He dealt with the responsibility of intellectuals in *Local Anaesthetic*, *From the Diary of a Snail* and in his "German tragedy" *The Plebeians Rehearse the Uprising*, and published political speeches and essays in which he advocated a Germany free from fanaticism and totalitarian ideologies. His childhood home, Danzig, and his broad and suggestive fabulations were to reappear in two successful novels criticising civilisation, *The Flounder* and *The Rat*, which reflect Grass's commitment to the peace movement and the environmental movement. Vehement debate and criticism were aroused by his mammoth novel *Ein weites Feld* which is set in the DDR in the years of the collapse of communism and the fall of the Berlin wall. *In My Century* he presents the history of the past century from a personal point of view, year by year. As a graphic artist, Grass has often been responsible for the covers and illustrations for his own works.

Grass was President of the Akademie der Künste in Berlin 1983–86, active within the German Authors' Publishing Company and PEN. He has been awarded a large number of prizes, among them Preis der Gruppe 47 1958, "Le meilleur livre étranger" 1962, the Büchner Prize 1965, the Fontane Prize 1968, Premio Internazionale Mondello 1977, the Alexander-Majakowski Medal, Gdansk 1979, the Antonio Feltrinelli Prize 1982, Großer Literaturpreis der Bayerischen Akademie 1994. He has honorary doctorates from Kenyon College and the Universities of Harvard, Poznan and Gdansk.

*A selection of works by Günter Grass in English:*

*The Tin Drum.* Transl. by Ralph Manheim. London: Secker & Warburg, 1962.
*Cat and Mouse.* Transl. by Ralph Manheim. San Diego: Harcourt Brace, 1963.
*Dog Years.* Transl. by Ralph Manheim. New York: Harcourt, Brace & World, 1965.
*Four Plays.* Introd. by Martin Esslin. New York: Harcourt, Brace & World, 1967.
*Speak out! Speeches, Open Letters, Commentaries.* Transl. by Ralph Manheim. London: Secker & Warburg, 1969.
*Local Anaesthetic.* Transl. by Ralph Manheim. New York: Harcourt, Brace & World, 1970.
*From the Diary of a Snail.* Transl. by Ralph Manheim. New York: Harcourt Brace Jovanovich, 1973.
*In the Egg and Other Poems.* Transl. by Michael Hamburger and Christopher Middleton. New York: Harcourt Brace Jovanovich, 1977.
*The Meeting at Telgte.* Transl. by Ralph Manheim. New York: Harcourt Brace Jovanovich, 1981.
*The Flounder.* Transl. by Ralph Manheim. New York: Harcourt Brace Jovanovich, 1978.
*Headbirths, or, the Germans are Dying Out.* Transl. by Ralph Manheim. New York: Harcourt Brace Jovanovich, 1982.
*The Rat.* Transl. by Ralph Manheim. San Diego: Harcourt Brace Jovanovich, 1987.
*Show Your Tongue.* Transl. by John E. Woods. San Diego: Harcourt Brace Jovanovich, 1987.
*Two States One Nation?* Transl. by Krishna Winston with A.S. Wensinger. San Diego: Harcourt Brace Jovanovich, 1990; London: Secker & Warburg.

*The Call of the Toad.* Transl. by Ralph Manheim. New York: Harcourt Brace Jovanovich, 1992.

*The Plebeians Rehearse the Uprising.* Transl. by Ralph Manheim. New York: Harcourt Brace, 1996.

*My Century.* Transl. by Michael Henry Heim. New York: Harcourt Brace, 1999.

*Too far afield.* Transl. by Krishna Winston. London: Faber, 2000.

# "TO BE CONTINUED ..."

Nobel Lecture, December 7, 1999
by
GÜNTER GRASS
Germany

Honoured Members of the Swedish Academy, Ladies and Gentlemen,

Having made this announcement, nineteenth-century works of fiction would go on and on. Magazines and newspapers gave them all the space they wished: the serialized novel was in its heyday. While the early chapters appeared in quick succession, the core of the work was being written out by hand, and its conclusion was yet to be conceived. Nor was it only trivial horror stories or tearjerkers that thus held the reader in thrall. Many of Dickens' novels came out in serial form, in instalments. Tolstoy's *Anna Karenina* was a serialized novel. Balzac's time, a tireless provider of mass-produced serializations, gave the still anonymous writer lessons in the technique of suspense, of building to climax at the end of a column. And nearly all Fontane's novels appeared first in newspapers and magazines as serializations. Witness the publisher of the *Vossische Zeitung*, where *Trials and Tribulations* first saw print, who exclaimed in a rage, "Will this sluttish story never end!"

But before I go on spinning these strands of my talk or move on to others, I wish to point out that from a purely literary point of view this hall and the Swedish Academy that invited me here are far from alien to me. My novel *The Rat*, which came out almost fourteen years ago and whose catastrophic course along various oblique levels of narration one or two of my readers may recall, features a eulogy delivered before just such an audience as you, an encomium to the rat or, to be more precise, the laboratory rat.

The rat has been awarded a Nobel Prize. At last, one might say. She's been on the list for years, even the short list. Representative of millions of experimental animals — from guinea pig to rhesus monkey — the white-haired, red-eyed laboratory rat is finally getting her due. For she more than anyone — or so claims the narrator of my novel — has made possible all the Nobelified research and discoveries in the field of medicine and, as far as Nobel laureates Watson and Crick are concerned, on the virtually boundless turf of gene manipulation. Since then maize and other vegetables — to say nothing of all sorts of animals — can be cloned more or less legally, which is why the rat-men, who increasingly take over as the novel comes to a close, that is, during the post-human era, are called Watsoncricks. They combine the best of both genera. Humans have much of the rat in them and vice versa. The world seems to use the synthesis to regain its health. After the Big Bang, when only rats, cockroaches, flies, and the remains of fish- and frog-eggs survive and it is time to make order out of the chaos, the Watsoncricks, who miraculously escape, do more than their share.

But since this strand of the narrative could as easily have ended with "To Be Continued ..." and the Nobel Prize speech in praise of the laboratory rat is certainly not meant to give the novel a happy end, I can now — as what might be called a matter of principle — turn to narration as a form of survival as well as a form of art.

People have always told tales. Long before humanity learned to write and gradually became literate, everybody told tales to everybody else and everybody listened to everybody else's tales. Before long it became clear that some of the still illiterate storytellers told more and better tales than others, that is, they could make more people believe their lies. And there were those among them who found artful ways of stemming the peaceful flow of their tales and diverting it into a tributary, that, far from drying up, turned suddenly and amazingly into a broad bed, though now full of flotsam and jetsam, the stuff of sub-plots. And because these primordial storytellers — who were not dependent upon day- or lamp-light and could carry on perfectly well in the dark, who were in fact adept at exploiting dusk or darkness to add to the suspense — because they stopped at nothing, neither dry stretches nor thundering waterfalls, except perhaps to interrupt the course of action with a "To Be Continued ..." if they sensed their audience's attention flagging, many of their listeners felt moved to start telling tales of their own.

What tales were told when no one could yet write and therefore no one wrote them down? From the days of Cain and Abel there were tales of murder and manslaughter. Feuds — blood feuds, in particular — were always good for a story. Genocide entered the picture quite early along with floods and droughts, fat years and lean years. Lengthy lists of cattle and slaves were perfectly acceptable, and no tale could be believable without detailed genealogies of who came before whom and who came after, heroic tales especially. Love triangles, popular even now, and tales of monsters — half man, half beast — who made their way through labyrinths or lay in wait in the bulrushes attracted mass audiences from the outset, to say nothing of legends of gods and idols and accounts of sea journeys, which were then handed down, polished, enlarged upon, modified, transmogrified into their opposites, and finally written down by a storyteller whose name was supposedly Homer or, in the case of the Bible, by a collective of storytellers. In China and Persia, in India and the Peruvian highlands, wherever writing flourished, storytellers — whether as groups or individuals, anonymously or by name — turned into literati.

Writing-fixated as we are, we nonetheless retain the memory of oral storytelling, the spoken origins of literature. And a good thing too, because if we were to forget that all storytelling comes through the lips — now inarticulate, hesitant, now swift, as if driven by fear, now in whisper, to keep the secrets revealed from reaching the wrong ears, now loudly and clearly, all the way from self-serving bluster to sniffing out the very essence of life — if our faith in writing were to make us forget all that, our storytelling would be bookish, dry as dust.

Yet how good too that we have so many books available to us and that whether we read them aloud or to ourselves they are permanent. They have been my inspiration. When I was young and malleable, masters like Melville and Döblin or Luther with his Biblical German prompted me to read aloud as I wrote, to mix ink with spit. Nor have things changed much since. Well into my fifth decade of enduring, no, relishing the moil and toil called writing, I chew tough, stringy clauses into manageable mush, babble to myself in blissful isolation, and put pen to paper only when I hear the proper tone and pitch, resonance and reverberation.

Yes, I love my calling. It keeps me company, a company whose polyphonic chatter calls for literal transcription into my manuscripts. And there is nothing I like more than to meet books of mine — books that have long since flown the coop and been expropriated by readers — when I read out loud to an audience what now lies peacefully on the page. For both the young, weaned early from language, and the old, grizzled yet still rapacious, the written word becomes spoken, and the magic works again and again. It is the shaman in the author earning a bit on the side, writing against the current of time, lying his way to tenable truths. And everyone believes his tacit promise: To Be Continued ...

But how did I become a writer, poet, and artist — all at once and all on frightening white paper? What homemade hubris put a child up to such craziness? After all, I was only twelve when I realized I wanted to be an artist. It coincided with the outbreak of the Second World War, when I was living on the outskirts of Danzig. But my first opportunity for professional development had to wait until the following year, when I found a tempting offer in the Hitler Youth magazine *Hilf mit!* (Lend a Hand). It was a story contest. With prizes. I immediately set to writing my first novel. Influenced by my mother's background, it bore the title *The Kashubians*, but the action did not take place in the painful present of that small and dwindling people; it took place in the thirteenth century during a period of interregnum, a grim period when brigands and robber barons ruled the highways and the only recourse a peasant had to justice was a kind of kangaroo court.

All I can remember of it is that after a brief outline of the economic conditions in the Kashubian hinterland I started in on pillages and massacres with a vengeance. There was so much throttling, stabbing, and skewering, so many kangaroo-court hangings and executions that by the end of the first chapter all the protagonists and a goodly number of the minor characters were dead and either buried or left to the crows. Since my sense of style did not allow me to turn corpses into spirits and the novel into a ghost story, I had to admit defeat with an abrupt end and no "To Be Continued ...". Not for good, of course, but the neophyte had learned his lesson: next time he would have to be a bit more gentle with his characters.

But first I read and read some more. I had my own way of reading: with my fingers in my ears. Let me say by way of explanation that my younger sister and I grew up in straitened circumstances, that is, in a two-room flat and hence without rooms of our own or even so much as a corner to ourselves. In the long run it turned out to be an advantage, though: I learned at an early age to concentrate in the midst of people or surrounded by noise. When I read I might have been under a bell jar; I was so involved in the world of the book that my mother, who liked a practical joke, once demonstrated her son's complete and utter absorption to a neighbour by replacing a roll I had been taking an occasional bite from with a bar of soap — Palmolive, I believe whereupon the two women — my mother not without a certain pride — watched me reach blindly for the soap, sink my teeth into it, and chew it for a good minute before it tore me away from my adventure on the page.

To this day I can concentrate as I did in my early years, but I have never read more obsessively. Our books were kept in a bookcase behind blue-curtained panes of glass. My mother belonged to a book club, and the novels of Dostoevsky and Tolstoy stood side by side and mixed in with novels by Hamsun, Raabe, and Vicki Baum. Selma Lagerlöf's *Gösta Berling* within easy reach. I later moved on to the Municipal Library, but my mother's collection provided the initial impulse. A punctilious businesswoman forced to sell her wares to unreliable customers on credit, she was also a great lover of beauty: she listened to opera and operetta melodies on her primitive radio, enjoyed hearing my promising stories, and frequently went to the Municipal Theatre, even taking me along from time to time.

The only reason I rehearse here these anecdotes of a petty bourgeois childhood after painting them with epic strokes decades ago in works peopled by fictitious characters is to help me answer the question "What made you become a writer?" The ability to daydream at length, the job of punning and playing with language in general, the addiction to lying for its own sake rather than for mine because sticking to the truth would have been a bore — in short, what is loosely known as talent was certainly a factor, but it was the abrupt intrusion of politics into the family idyll that turned the all too flighty category of talent into a ballast with a certain permanence and depth.

My mother's favourite cousin, like her a Kashubian by birth, worked at the Polish post office of the Free City of Danzig. He was a regular at our house and always welcome. When the War broke out the Hevelius Square post office building held out for a time against the SS-Heimwehr, and my uncle was rounded up with those who finally surrendered. They were tried summarily and put before a firing squad. Suddenly he was no more. Suddenly and permanently his name was no longer mentioned. He became a non-person. Yet he must have lived on in me through the years when at fifteen I donned a uniform, at sixteen I learned what fear was, at seventeen I landed in an American POW camp, at eighteen I worked in the black market, studied to be a stone-mason and started sculpting in stone, prepared for admission to art school, and wrote and drew, drew and wrote, fleet-footed verse, quizzical one-acts, and on it went until I found the material unwieldy — I seem to have an inborn need for aesthetic pleasure. And beneath the detritus of it all lay my mother's favourite cousin, the Polish postal clerk, shot and buried, only to be found by me (who else?) and exhumed and resuscitated by literary artificial respiration under other names and guises, though this time in a novel whose major and minor characters, full of life and beans as they are, make it through a number of chapters, some even holding out till the end and thus enabling the writer to keep his recurrent promise: To Be Continued ...

And so on and so forth. The publication of my first two novels, *The Tin Drum* and *Dog Years*, and the novella I stuck between them, *Cat and Mouse*, taught me early on, as a relatively young writer, that books can cause offence, stir up fury, even hatred, that what is undertaken out of love for one's country can be taken as soiling one's nest. From then on I have been controversial.

Which means that like writers banished to Siberia or suchlike places I am in good company. So I have no grounds to complain; on the contrary, writers should consider the condition of permanent controversiality to be invigorating, part of the risk involved in choosing the profession. It is a fact of life that writers have always and with due consideration and great pleasure spit in the soup of the high and mighty. That is what makes the history of literature analogous to the development and refinement of censorship.

The ill humour of the powers-that-be forced Socrates to drain the cup of hemlock to the dregs, sent Ovid into exile, made Seneca open his veins. For centuries and to the present day the finest fruits of the western garden of literature have graced the index of the Catholic church. How much equivocation did the European Enlightenment learn from the censorship practised by princes with absolute power? How many German, Italian, Spanish, and Portuguese writers did fascism drive from their lands and languages? How many writers fell victim to the Leninist-Stalinist reign of terror? And what constraints are writers under today in countries like China, Kenya, or Croatia?

I come from the land of book-burning. We know that the desire to destroy a hated book is still (or once more) part of the spirit of our times and that when necessary it finds appropriate telegenic expression and therefore a mass audience. What is much worse, however, is that the persecution of writers, including the threat of murder and murder itself, is on the rise throughout the world, so much so that the world has grown accustomed to the terror of it. True, the part of the world that calls itself free raises a hue and cry when, as in 1995 in Nigeria, a writer like Ken Saro-Wiwa and his supporters are sentenced to death and killed for taking a stand against the contamination of their country, but things immediately go back to normal, because ecological considerations might affect the profits of the world's number one oil colossus Shell.

What makes books — and with them writers — so dangerous that church and state, politburos and the mass media feel the need to oppose them? Silencing and worse are seldom the result of direct attacks on the reigning ideology. Often all it takes is a literary allusion to the idea that truth exist only in the plural — that there is no such thing as a single truth but only a multitude of truths — to make the defenders of one or another truth sense danger, mortal danger. Then there is the problem that writers are by definition unable to leave the past in peace: they are quick to open closed wounds, peer behind closed doors, find skeletons in the cupboard, consume sacred cows or, as in the case of Jonathan Swift, offer up Irish children, "stewed, roasted, baked, or boiled", to the kitchens of the English nobility. In other words, nothing is sacred to them, not even capitalism, and that makes them offensive, even criminal. But worst of all they refuse to make common cause with the victors of history: they take pleasure milling about the fringes of the historical process with the losers, who have plenty to say but no platform to say it on. By giving them a voice, they call the victory into question, by associating with them, they join ranks with them.

Of course the powers-that-be, no matter what period costume they may be wearing, have nothing against literature as such. They enjoy it as an ornament and even promote it. At present its role is to entertain, to serve the fun culture, to de-emphasize the negative side of things and give people hope, a light in the darkness. What is basically called for, though not quite so explicitly as during the Communist years, is a "positive hero". In the jungle of the free market economy he is likely to pave his way to success Rambo-like with corpses and a smile; he is an adventurer who is always up for a quick fuck between battles, a winner who leaves a trail of losers behind him, in short, the perfect role model for our globalized world. And the demand for the hard-boiled he-man who always lands on his feet is unfailingly met by the media: James Bond has spawned any number of Dolly-like children. Good will continue to prevail over evil as long as it assumes his cool-guy pose.

Does that make his opposite or enemy a negative hero? Not necessarily. I have my roots, as you will have noticed from your reading, in the Spanish or Moorish school of the picaresque novel. Tilting at windmills has remained a model for that school down through the ages, and the picaro's very existence derives from the comic nature of defeat. He pees on the pillars of power and saws away at the throne knowing full well he will make no dent in either: once he moves on, the exalted temple may look a bit shabby, the throne may wobble slightly, but that is all. His humour is part and parcel of his despair. While *Die Götterdämmerung* drones on before an elegant Bayreuth audience, he sits sniggering in the back row, because in his theatre comedy and tragedy go hand in hand. He scorns the fateful march of the victors and sticks his foot out to trip them, yet much as his failure makes us laugh the laughter sticks in our throat: even his wittiest cynicisms have a tragic cast to them. Besides, from the point of view of the philistine, rightist or leftist, he is a formalist — even a mannerist — of the first order: he holds the spyglass the wrong way; he sees time as a train on a siding: he puts mirrors everywhere; you can never tell whose ventriloquist he is; given his perspective, he can even accept dwarfs and giants into his entourage. The reason Rabelais was constantly on the run from the secular police and the Holy Inquisition is that his larger-than-life Gargantua and Pantagruel had turned the world according to scholasticism on its head. The laughter they unleashed was positively infernal. When Gargantua stooped bare-arsed on the towers of Notre-Dame and pissed the length and breadth of Paris under water, everyone who did not drown guffawed. Or to go back to Swift: his modest culinary proposal for relieving the hunger in Ireland could be brought up to date if at the next economic summit the board set for the heads of state were groaning with lusciously prepared street children from Brazil or southern Sudan. Satire is the name of the art form I have in mind, and in satire everything is permitted, even tickling the funny bone with the grotesque.

When Heinrich Böll gave his Nobel lecture here on 2 May 1973, he brought the seemingly opposing positions of reason and poetry into closer and closer proximity and bemoaned the lack of time to go into another aspect of the issue: "I have had to pass over humour, which, though no class privilege, is ignored in his poetry as a hiding place for resistance." Now Böll knew that Jean Paul, the poet in question, had a place in the German Culture Hall of Fame, little read though he is nowadays; he knew to what extent Thomas Mann's literary oeuvre was suspected — by both the right and the left — of irony at the time (and still is, I might add). Clearly what Böll had in mind was not belly-laugh humour but rather inaudible, between-the-lines humour, the chronic susceptibility to melancholy of his clown, the desperate wit of the man who collected silence, an activity, by the way, that has become quite the thing in the media and — under the guise of "voluntary self-control" on the part of the free West — a benign disguise for censorship.

By the early fifties, when I had started writing consciously, Heinrich Böll was a well-known if not always well-received author. With Wolfgang Koeppen, Günter Eich, and Arno Schmidt he stood apart from the culture industry. Post-war German literature, still young, was having a hard time with German, which had been corrupted by the Nazi regime. In addition, Böll's generation — but also the younger writers like myself — were stymied to a certain extent by a prohibition that came from Theodor Adorno: "It is barbaric to write a poem after Auschwitz, and that is why it has become impossible to write poetry to-day ..."

In other words, no more "To Be Continued ..." Though write we did. We wrote by bearing in mind, like Adorno in his *Minima Moralia: Reflections from Damaged Life* (1951), that Auschwitz marks a rift, an unbridgeable gap in the history of civilization. It was the only way we could get round the prohibition. Even so, Adorno's writing on the wall has retained its power to this day. All the writers of my generation did public battle with it. No one had the desire or ability to keep silent. It was our duty to take the goosestep out of German, to lure it out of its idylls and fogged inwardness. We, the children who had had our fingers burned, we were the ones to repudiate the absolutes, the ideological black or white. Doubt and scepticism were our godparents and the multitude of gray values their present to us. In any case, such was the asceticism I imposed on myself before discovering the richness of a language I had all too sweepingly pronounced guilty: its seducible softness, its tendency to plumb the depths, its utterly supple hardness, not to mention the sheen of its dialects, its artless- and artfulness, its eccentricities, and beauty blossoming from its subjunctives. Having won back this capital, we invested it to make more. Despite Adorno's verdict or spurred on by it. The only way writing after Auschwitz, poetry or prose, could proceed was by becoming memory and preventing the past from coming to an end. Only then could post-war literature in German justify applying the generally valid "To Be Continued …" to itself and its descendants; only then could the wound be kept open and the much desired and prescribed forgetting be reversed with a steadfast "Once upon a time".

How many times when one or another interest group calls for considering what happened a closed chapter — we need to return to normalcy and put our shameful past behind us — how many times has literature resisted. And rightly so! Because it is a position as foolish as it is understandable; because every time the end of the post-war period is proclaimed in Germany — as it was ten years ago, with the Wall down and unity in the offing — the past catches up with us.

At that time, in February 1990, I gave a talk to students in Frankfurt entitled "Writing After Auschwitz". I wanted to take stock of my works book by book. In *The Diary of a Snail,* which came out in 1972 and in which past and present crisscross, but also run parallel or occasionally collide, I am asked by my sons how I define my profession, and I answer, "A writer, children, is someone who writes against the current of time." What I said to the students was: "Such a view presumes that writers are not encapsulated in isolation or the sempiternal, that they see themselves as living in the here and now, and, even more, that they expose themselves to the vicissitudes of time, that they jump in and take sides. The dangers of jumping in and taking sides are well known: The distance a writer is supposed to keep is threatened; his language must live from hand to mouth; the narrowness of current events can make him narrow and curb the imagination he has trained to run free; he runs the danger of running out of breath."

The risk I referred to then has remained with me throughout the years. But what would the profession of writer be like without risk? Granted, the writer would have the security of, say, a cultural bureaucrat, but he would be the prisoner of his fears of dirtying his hands with the present. Out of fear of losing his distance he would lose himself in realms where myths reside and lofty thoughts are all. But the present, which the past is constantly turning into, would catch up to him in the end and put him through the third degree. Because every writer is of his time, no matter how he protests being born too early or late. He does not autonomously choose what he will write about, that choice is made for him. At least I was not free to choose. Left to my own devices, I would have followed the laws of aesthetics and been perfectly happy to seek my place in texts droll and harmless.

But that was not to be. There were extenuating circumstances: mountains of rubble and cadavers, fruit of the womb of German history. The more I shovelled, the more it grew. It simply could not be ignored. Besides, I come from a family of refugees, which means that in addition to everything that drives a writer from book to book — common ambition, the fear of boredom, the mechanisms of egocentricity — I had the irreparable loss of my birthplace. If by telling tales I could not recapture a city both lost and destroyed, I could at least re-conjure it. And this obsession kept me going. I wanted to make it clear to myself and my readers, not without a bit of a chip on my shoulder, that what was lost did not need to sink into oblivion, that it could be resuscitated by the art of literature in all its grandeur and pettiness: the churches and cemeteries, the sounds of the shipyards and smells of the faintly lapping Baltic, a language on its way out yet still stable-warm and grumble-rich, sins in need of confession, and crimes tolerated if never exonerated.

A similar loss has provided other writers with a hotbed of obsessive topics. In a conversation dating back many years Salman Rushdie and I concurred that my lost Danzig was for me — like his lost Bombay for him — both resource and refuse pit, point of departure and navel of the world. This arrogance, this overkill lies at the very heart of literature. It is the condition for a story that can pull out all the stops. Painstaking detail, sensitive psychologizing, slice-of-life realism — no such techniques can handle our monstrous raw materials. As indebted as we are to the Enlightenment tradition of reason, the absurd course of history spurns all exclusively reasonable explanations.

Just as the Nobel Prize — once we divest it of its ceremonial garb — has its roots in the invention of dynamite, which like such other human headbirths as the splitting of the atom and the likewise Nobelified classification of the gene has wrought both weal and woe in the world, so literature has an explosive quality at its root, though the explosions literature releases have a delayed-action effect and change the world only in the magnifying glass of time, so to speak, it too wreaking cause for both joy and lamentation here below. How long did it take the European Enlightenment from Montaigne to Voltaire, Diderot, Kant, Lessing, and Lichtenberg to introduce a flicker of reason into the dark corners of scholasticism? And even that flicker often died in the process, a process censorship went a long way towards inhibiting. But when the light finally did brighten things up, it turned out to be the light of cold reason, limited to the technically doable, to economic and social progress, a reason that claimed to be enlightened but that merely drummed a reason-based jargon (which amounted to instructions for making progress at all costs) into its offspring, capitalism and socialism (which were at each other's throats from the word go).

Today we can see what those brilliant failures who were the Enlightenment's offspring have wrought. We can see what a dangerous position its delayed-action, word-detonated explosion has hurled us into. And if we are trying to repair the damage with Enlightenment tools, it is only because we have no others. We look on in horror as capitalism — now that his brother, socialism, has been declared dead — rages unimpeded, megalomaniacally replaying the errors of the supposedly extinct brother. It has turned the free market into dogma, the only truth, and intoxicated by its all but limitless power, plays the wildest of games, making merger after merger with no goal than to maximize profits. No wonder capitalism is proving as impervious to reform as the communism that managed to strangle itself. Globalization is its motto, a motto it proclaims with the arrogance of infallibility: there is no alternative.

Accordingly, history has come to an end. No more "To Be Continued ...", no more suspense. Though perhaps there is hope that if not politics, which has abdicated its decision-making power to economics, then at least literature may come up with something to cause the "new dogmatism" to falter.

How can subversive writing be both dynamite and of literary quality? Is there time enough to wait for the delayed action? Is any book capable of supplying a commodity in so short supply as the future? Is it not rather the case that literature is currently retreating from public life and that young writers are using the internet as a playground? A standstill, to which the suspicious word "communication" lends a certain aura, is making headway. Every scrap of time is planned down to the last nervous breakdown. A cultural industry vale of tears is taking over the world. What is to be done?

My godlessness notwithstanding, all I can do is bend my knee to a saint who has never failed me and cracked some of the hardest nuts. "O Holy and (through the grace of Camus) Nobelified Sisyphus! May thy stone not remain at the top of the hill, may we roll it down again and like thee continue to rejoice in it, and may the story told of the drudgery of our existence have no end. Amen."

But will my prayer be heard? Or are the rumours true? Is the new breed of cloned creature destined to assure the continuation of human history?

Which brings me back to the beginning of my talk. Once more I open *The Rat* to the fifth chapter, in which the laboratory rat, representing millions of other laboratory animals in the cause of research, wins the Nobel Prize, and I am reminded how few prizes have been awarded to projects that would rid the world of the scourge of mankind: hunger. Anyone who can pay the price can get a new pair of kidneys. Hearts can be transplanted. We can phone anywhere in the world wire-free. Satellites and space stations orbit us solicitously. The latest weapon systems, conceived and developed, they too, on the basis of award-winning research, can help their masters to keep death at bay. Anything the human mind comes up with finds astonishing applications. Only hunger seems to resist. It is even increasing. Poverty deeply rooted shades into misery. Refugees are flocking all over the world accompanied by hunger. It takes political will paired with scientific know-how to root out misery of such magnitude, and no one seems resolved to undertake it.

In 1973, just when terror — with the active support of the United States — was beginning to strike in Chile, Willy Brandt spoke before the United Nations General Assembly, the first German chancellor to do so. He brought up the issue of worldwide poverty. The applause following his exclamation "Hunger too is war!" was stunning.

I was present when he gave the speech. I was working on my novel *The Flounder* at the time. It deals with the very foundations of human existence including food, the lack and superabundance thereof, great gluttons and untold starvelings, the joys of the palate and crusts from the rich man's table.

The issue is still with us. The poor counter growing riches with growing birth rates. The affluent north and west can try to screen themselves off in security-mad fortresses, but the flocks of refugees will catch up with them: no gate can withstand the crush of the hungry.

The future will have something to say about all this. Our common novel must be continued. And even if one day people stop or are forced to stop writing and publishing, if books are no longer available, there will still be storytellers giving us mouth-to-ear artificial respiration, spinning old stories in new ways: loud and soft, heckling and halting, now close to laughter, now on the brink of tears.

*Translated from German by Michael Henry Heim*

Literature 2000

## GAO XINGJIAN

*"for an oeuvre of universal validity, bitter insights and linguistic ingenuity, which has opened new paths for the Chinese novel and drama"*

# THE NOBEL PRIZE IN LITERATURE

Speech by Professor Göran Malmqvist of the Swedish Academy. Translation of the Swedish text.

Your Majesties, Your Royal Highnesses, Ladies and Gentlemen,

Gao Xingjian's literary output comprises eighteen plays, two great novels, and a number of stories, which all fit in one volume. Born in 1940, he began his career as a writer as early as the sixties. His production would certainly have been much larger had not the conditions of life during the Cultural Revolution forced him to burn all his manuscripts of the sixties and the seventies. He also made very important contributions to the theoretical debate concerning the structure and functions of drama and the novel in China during the eighties. His work as a breaker of new ground relates to the form and structure of a literary work as well as to its psychological foundations.

The novel called *Soul Mountain* (1990) stands out as one of the foremost works in twentieth-century Chinese literature. Among many other things Gao Xingjian deals in it with an existential dilemma: man's urge to find the absolute independence granted by solitude conflicts with a longing for the warmth and fellowship which can be given by "the other," be it he or she. At the same time, however, this enriching companionship threatens the individual's integrity and, without fail, ends in some kind of struggle for power.

The author's vivid sense of alienation in a politics-ridden society made him, in the early eighties, go in search for hidden-away parts of southwestern and southern China, where there still existed traces of primitive cultures, age-old shamanistic rites and Daoist notions. In his portrayal of these cultures, replete with fantastic cock-and-bull stories which bring to the reader's mind the repertoires of traditional storytellers, he also castigates strict Confucian orthodoxy as well as Marxist ideology and their respective demands for obedience and uniformity.

In the course of his pilgrimage to Soul Mountain, where he hopes to find the ultimate truth about the meaning of life and the human condition, the author's ego is stricken by loneliness and is forced into creating a *you*, a projection of itself, which, in turn, hit by the same loneliness, creates a *she*. The numerous *he* figures that make their appearance in the novel are likewise projections of the author's ego. With the help of these pronominal projections, the author manages to investigate a wide range of human relationships and their consequences for the individual.

The novel entitled *One Man's Bible* (1999), which Gao Xingjian himself looks upon as a companion novel to *Soul Mountain*, is a novel of confession in which he mercilessly lays bare the three different parts he played during the Cultural Revolution: as a leader of a rebel faction, as a victim and as a silent observer. Again he makes use of the pronouns *you* and *he* in order to distinguish between two different degrees of alienation: *you* stands for the exiled author *here* and *now*, *he* is the author *there* and *then*, in the China of the Cultural Revolution. The framing chapters, which describe episodes in the author's exiled existence, are as factual and personally revealing as those dealing with his different roles during the Cultural Revolution. It is these framing chapters that enable the author to give his view on the meaning of human existence, the nature of literature, the conditions of authorship and, first and foremost, on the importance of remembering and of imagination for the author's view of reality.

The foundation for Gao Xingjian's pioneering activity as a dramatist was laid in the first half of the nineteen-eighties when he worked as artistic advisor, director of plays and playwright at the People's Art Theatre in Peking, at that time considered to be the country's foremost stage. Gao Xingjian's plays are characterized by originality, in no way diminished by the fact that he has been influenced both by modern Western and traditional Chinese currents. His greatness as a dramatist lies in the manner in which he has succeeded in enriching these fundamentally different elements and making them coalesce to something entirely new.

Dear Gao Xingjian,

You did not leave China empty-handed. You have come to look on the native language which you brought with you when you left China as your true and real country. It gives me great joy to offer you, on behalf of the Swedish Academy, our warmest congratulations. I will ask you now to receive, from the hands of His Majesty the King, this year's Nobel Prize for Literature.

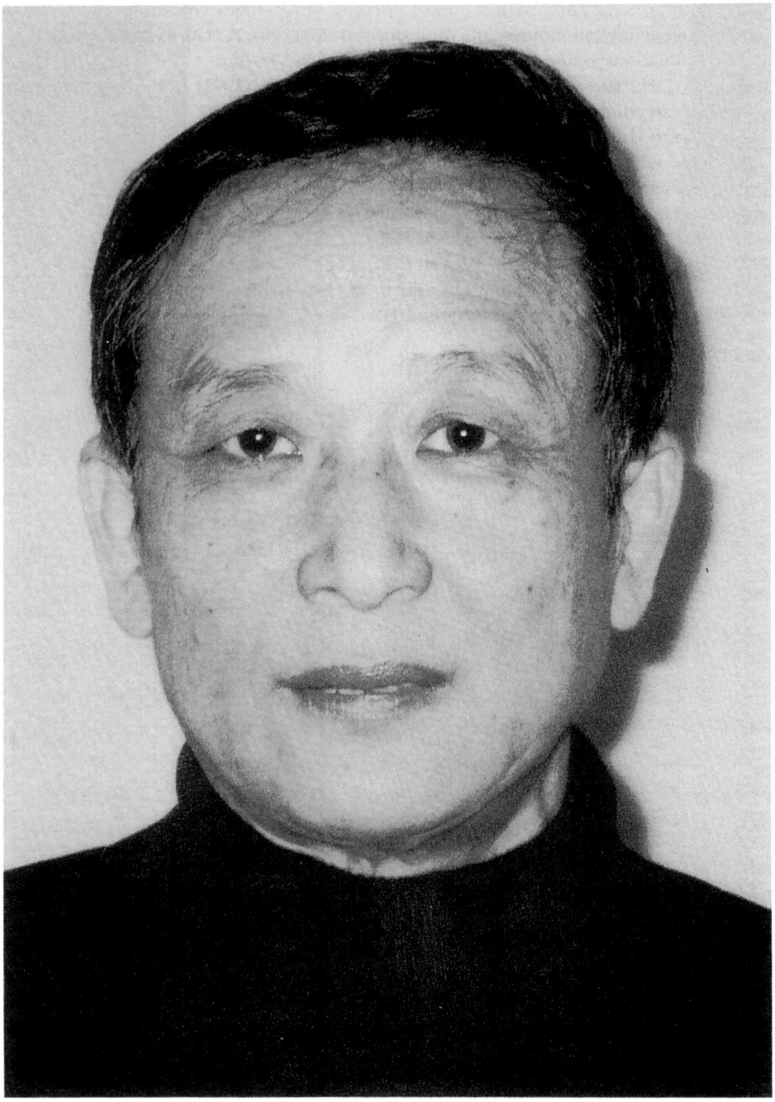

高行健

# GAO XINGJIAN

Gao Xingjian, born January 4, 1940 in Ganzhou (Jiangxi province) in eastern China, is today a French citizen. Writer of prose, translator, dramatist, director, critic and artist. Gao Xingjian grew up during the aftermath of the Japanese invasion, his father was a bank official and his mother an amateur actress who stimulated the young Gao's interest in the theatre and writing. He received his basic education in the schools of the People's Republic and took a degree in French in 1962 at the Department of Foreign Languages in Beijing. During the Cultural Revolution (1966–76) he was sent to a re-education camp and felt it necessary to burn a suitcase full of manuscripts. Not until 1979 could he publish his work and travel abroad, to France and Italy. During the period 1980–87 he published short stories, essays and dramas in literary magazines in China and also four books: *Premier essai sur les techniques du roman moderne/A Preliminary Discussion of the Art of Modern Fiction* (1981) which gave rise to a violent polemic on "modernism", the narrative *A Pigeon Called Red Beak* (1985), *Collected Plays* (1985) and *In Search of a Modern Form of Dramatic Representation* (1987). Several of his experimental and pioneering plays — inspired in part by Brecht, Artaud and Beckett — were produced at the Theatre of Popular Art in Beijing: his theatrical debut with *Signal d'alarme/Signal Alarm* (1982) was a tempestuous success, and the absurd drama which established his reputation *Arrêt de bus/Bus Stop* (1983) was condemned during the campaign against "intellectual pollution" (described by one eminent member of the party as the most pernicious piece of writing since the foundation of the People's Republic); *L'Homme sauvage/Wild Man* (1985) also gave rise to heated domestic polemic and international attention.

In 1986 *L'autre rive/The Other Shore* was banned and since then none of his plays have been performed in China. In order to avoid harassment he undertook a ten-month walking-tour of the forest and mountain regions of Sichuan Province, tracing the course of the Yangzi river from its source to the coast. In 1987 he left China and settled down a year later in Paris as a political refugee. After the massacre on the Square of Heavenly Peace in 1989 he left the Chinese Communist Party. After publication of *La fuite/Fugitives*, which takes place against the background of this massacre, he was declared *persona non grata* by the regime and his works were banned. In the summer of 1982, Gao Xingjian had already started working on his prodigious novel *La Montagne de l'Âme/Soul Mountain*, in which — by means of an odyssey in time and space through the Chinese countryside — he enacts an individual's search for roots, inner peace and liberty. This is supplemented by the more autobiographical *Le Livre d'un homme seul/One Man's Bible*.

A number of his works have been translated into various languages, and today several of his plays are being produced in various parts of the world. In Sweden he has been translated and introduced by Göran Malmqvist, and two of his plays (*Summer Rain in Peking*, *Fugitives*) have been performed at the Royal Dramatic Theatre in Stockholm.

Gao Xingjian paints in ink and has had some thirty international exhibitions and provides the cover illustrations for his own books.

Awards: Chevalier de l'Ordre des Arts et des Lettres 1992; Prix Communauté française de Belgique 1994 (for *Le somnambule*), Prix du Nouvel An chinois 1997 (for *Soul Mountain*).

*A selection of works by Gao Xingjian in English:*

*Wild Man: A Contemporary Chinese Spoken Drama.* Transl. and annotated by Bruno Roubicek. Asian Theatre Journal. Vol. 7, Nr 2. Fall 1990.
*Fugitives.* Transl. by Gregory B. Lee. In: Lee, Gregory B., *Chinese Writing and Exile.* Central Chinese Studies of the Universtity of Chicago, 1993.
*The Other Shore: Plays by Gao Xingjian.* Transl. by Gilbert C.F. Fong. Hong Kong: The Chinese University Press, 1999.
*Soul Mountain.* Transl. by Mabel Lee. HarperCollins, 1999.
*One Man's Bible.* Transl. by Mabel Lee. HarperCollins, 2002.
*Contemporary Technique and National Character in Fiction.* Transl. by Ng Mau-sang.
[Extract from *A Preliminary Discussion of the Art of Modern Fiction,* 1981.]
"The Voice of the Individual". *Stockholm Journal of East Asian Studies* 6, 1995.
"Without isms". Transl. by W. Lau, D. Sauviat & M. Williams. *Journal of the Oriental Society of Australia.* Vols. 27 & 28, 1995–96.

# THE CASE FOR LITERATURE

Nobel Lecture, December 7, 2000
by
GAO XINGJIAN
France

I have no way of knowing whether it was fate that has pushed me onto this dais but as various lucky coincidences have created this opportunity I may as well call it fate. Putting aside discussion of the existence or non-existence of God, I would like to say that despite my being an atheist I have always shown reverence for the unknowable.

A person cannot be God, certainly not replace God, and rule the world as a Superman; he will only succeed in creating more chaos and make a greater mess of the world. In the century after Nietzsche man-made disasters left the blackest records in the history of humankind. Supermen of all types called leader of the people, head of the nation and commander of the race did not baulk at resorting to various violent means in perpetrating crimes that in no way resemble the ravings of a very egotistic philosopher. However, I do not wish to waste this talk on literature by saying too much about politics and history; what I want to do is to use this opportunity to speak as one writer in the voice of an individual.

A writer is an ordinary person, perhaps he is more sensitive but people who are highly sensitive are often more frail. A writer does not speak as the spokesperson of the people or as the embodiment of righteousness. His voice is inevitably weak but it is precisely this voice of the individual that is more authentic.

What I want to say here is that literature can only be the voice of the individual and this has always been so. Once literature is contrived as the hymn of the nation, the flag of the race, the mouthpiece of a political party or the voice of a class or a group, it can be employed as a mighty and all-engulfing tool of propaganda; However, such literature loses what is inherent in literature, ceases to be literature, and becomes a substitute for power and profit.

In the century just ended literature confronted precisely this misfortune and was more deeply scarred by politics and power than in any previous period, and the writer too was subjected to unprecedented oppression.

In order that literature safeguard the reason for its own existence and not become the tool of politics it must return to the voice of the individual, for literature is primarily derived from the feelings of the individual and is the result of feelings. This is not to say that literature must therefore be divorced from politics or that it must necessarily be involved in politics. Controversies about literary trends or a writer's political inclinations were serious afflictions that tormented literature during the past century. Ideology wreaked havoc by turning related controversies over tradition and reform into controversies over what was conservative or revolutionary and thus changed literary issues into a struggle over what was progressive or reactionary. If ideology unites with power and is transformed into a real force then both literature and the individual will be destroyed.

Chinese literature in the twentieth century time and again was worn out and indeed almost suffocated because politics dictated literature: both the revolution in literature and revolutionary literature alike passed death sentences on literature and the individual. The attack on Chinese traditional culture in the name of the revolution resulted in the public prohibition and burning of books. Countless writers were shot, imprisoned, exiled or punished with hard labour in the course of the past one hundred years. This was more extreme than in any imperial dynastic period of China's history, creating enormous difficulties for writings in the Chinese language and even more for any discussion of creative freedom.

If the writer sought to win intellectual freedom the choice was either to fall silent or to flee. However the writer relies on language and not to speak for a prolonged period is the same as suicide. The writer who sought to avoid suicide or being silenced and furthermore to express his own voice had no option but to go into exile. Surveying the history of literature in the East and the West this has always been so: from Qu Yuan to Dante, Joyce, Thomas Mann, Solzhenitsyn, and to the large numbers of Chinese intellectuals who went into exile after the Tiananmen massacre in 1989. This is the inevitable fate of the poet and the writer who continues to seek to preserve his own voice.

During the years when Mao Zedong implemented total dictatorship even fleeing was not an option. The monasteries on far away mountains that provided refuge for scholars in feudal times were totally ravaged and to write even in secret was to risk one's life. To maintain one's intellectual autonomy one could only talk to oneself, and it had to be in utmost secrecy. I should mention that it was only in this period when it was utterly impossible for literature that I came to comprehend why it was so essential: literature allows a person to preserve a human consciousness.

It can be said that talking to oneself is the starting point of literature and that using language to communicate is secondary. A person pours his feelings and thoughts into language that, written as words, becomes literature. At the time there is no thought of utility or that some day it might be published yet there is the compulsion to write because there is recompense and consolation in the pleasure of writing. I began writing my novel *Soul Mountain* to dispel my inner loneliness at the very time when works I had written with rigorous self-censorship had been banned. *Soul Mountain* was written for myself and without the hope that it would be published.

From my experience in writing, I can say that literature is inherently man's affirmation of the value of his own self and that this is validated during the writing: literature is born primarily of the writer's need for self-fulfilment. Whether it has any impact on society comes after the completion of a work and that impact certainly is not determined by the wishes of the writer.

In the history of literature there are many great enduring works which were not published in the lifetimes of the authors. If the authors had not achieved self-affirmation while writing, how could they have continued to write? As in the case of Shakespeare, even now it is difficult to ascertain the details of the lives of the four geniuses who wrote China's greatest novels, *Journey to the West, Water Margin, Jin Ping Mei* and *Dream of Red Mansions*. All that remains is an autobiographical essay by Shi Naian and had he not as he said consoled himself by writing, how else could he have devoted the rest of his life to that huge work for which he received no recompense during life? And was this not also the case with Kafka who pioneered modern fiction and with Fernando Pessoa the most profound poet of the twentieth century? Their turning to language was not in order to reform the world and while profoundly aware of the helplessness of the individual they still spoke out, for such is the magic of language.

Language is the ultimate crystallisation of human civilisation. It is intricate, incisive and difficult to grasp, and yet it is pervasive, penetrates human perceptions and links man, the perceiving subject, to his own understanding of the world. The written word is also magical for it allows communication between separate individuals, even if they are from different races and times. It is also in this way that the shared present time in the writing and reading of literature is connected to its eternal spiritual value.

In my view, for a writer of the present to strive to emphasise a national culture is problematical. Because of where I was born and the language I use, the cultural traditions of China naturally reside within me. Culture and language are always closely related, and thus characteristic and relatively stable modes of perception, thought and articulation are formed. However a writer's creativity begins precisely with what has already been articulated in his language and addresses what has not been adequately articulated in that language. As the creator of linguistic art there is no need to stick on oneself a stock national label that can be easily recognised.

Literature transcends national boundaries — through translations it transcends languages and then specific social customs and inter-human relationships created by geographical location and history — to make profound revelations about the universality of human nature. Furthermore, the writer today receives multicultural influences outside the culture of his own race so, unless it is to promote tourism, emphasising the cultural features of a people is inevitably suspect.

Literature transcends ideology, national boundaries and racial consciousness in the same way as the individual's existence basically transcends this or that -ism. This is because man's existential condition is superior to any theories or speculations about life. Literature is a universal observation on the dilemmas of human existence and nothing is taboo. Restrictions on literature are always externally imposed: politics, society, ethics and customs set out to tailor literature into decorations for their various frameworks.

However, literature is neither an embellishment for authority or a socially fashionable item, it has its own criterion of merit: its aesthetic quality. An aesthetic intricately related to the human emotions is the only indispensable criterion for literary works. Indeed, such judgements differ from person to person because the emotions are invariably that of different individuals. However, such subjective aesthetic judgements do have universally recognised standards. The capacity for critical appreciation nurtured by literature allows the reader to also experience the poetic feeling and the beauty, the sublime and the ridiculous, the sorrow and the absurdity, and the humour and the irony that the author has infused into his work.

Poetic feeling does not derive simply from the expression of the emotions; nevertheless, unbridled egotism, a form of infantilism, is difficult to avoid in the early stages of writing. Also, there are numerous levels of emotional expression and to reach higher levels requires cold detachment. Poetry is concealed in the distanced gaze. Furthermore, if this gaze also examines the person of the author and overarches both the characters of the book and the author to become the author's third eye, one that is as neutral as possible, the disasters and the refuse of the human world will all be worthy of scrutiny. Then as feelings of pain, hatred and abhorrence are aroused, so too are feelings of concern and love for life.

An aesthetic based on human emotions does not become outdated even with the perennial changing of fashions in literature and in art. However, literary evaluations that fluctuate like fashions are premised on what is the latest: that is, whatever is new is good. This is a mechanism in general market movements and the book market is not exempted, but if the writer's aesthetic judgement follows market movements it will mean the suicide of literature. Especially in the so-called consumerist society of the present, I think one must resort to cold literature.

Ten years ago, after concluding *Soul Mountain* which I had written over seven years, I wrote a short essay proposing this type of literature:

"Literature is not concerned with politics but is purely a matter of the individual. It is the gratification of the intellect together with an observation, a review of what has been experienced, reminiscences and feelings or the portrayal of a state of mind."

"The so-called writer is nothing more than someone speaking or writing and whether he is listened to or read is for others to choose. The writer is not a hero acting on orders from the people nor is he worthy of worship as an idol, and certainly he is not a criminal or enemy of the people. He is at times victimised along with his writings simply because of others' needs. When the authorities need to manufacture a few enemies to divert people's attention, writers become sacrifices, and worse still writers who have been duped actually think it is a great honour to be sacrificed."

"In fact the relationship of the author and the reader is always one of spiritual communication and there is no need to meet or to socially interact; it is a communication simply through the work. Literature remains an indispensable form of human activity in which both the reader and the writer are engaged of their own volition. Hence, literature has no duty to the masses."

"This sort of literature that has recovered its innate character can be called cold literature. It exists simply because humankind seeks a purely spiritual activity beyond the gratification of material desires. This sort of literature of course did not come into being today. However, whereas in the past it mainly had to fight oppressive political forces and social customs, today it has to do battle with the subversive commercial values of consumerist society. For it to exist depends on a willingness to endure the loneliness."

"If a writer devotes himself to this sort of writing he will find it difficult to make a living. Hence the writing of this sort of literature must be considered a luxury, a form of pure spiritual gratification. If this sort of literature has the good fortune of being published and circulated it is due to the efforts of the writer and his friends; Cao Xueqin and Kafka are such examples. During their lifetimes, their works were unpublished so they were not able to create literary movements or to become celebrities. These writers lived at the margins and seams of society, devoting themselves to this sort of spiritual activity for which at the time they did not hope for any recompense. They did not seek social approval but simply derived pleasure from writing."

"Cold literature is literature that will flee in order to survive; it is literature that refuses to be strangled by society in its quest for spiritual salvation. If a race cannot accommodate this sort of non-utilitarian literature it is not merely a misfortune for the writer but a tragedy for the race."

It is my good fortune to be receiving, during my lifetime, this great honour from the Swedish Academy, and in this I have been helped by many friends from all over the world. For years without thought of reward and not shirking difficulties they have translated, published, performed and evaluated my writings. However I will not thank them one by one for it is a very long list of names.

I should also thank France for accepting me. In France where literature and art are revered I have won the conditions to write with freedom, and I also have readers and audiences. Fortunately I am not lonely although writing, to which I have committed myself, is a solitary affair.

What I would also like to say here is that life is not a celebration and that the rest of the world is not peaceful as in Sweden, where for one hundred and eighty years there has been no war. This new century will not be immune to catastrophes simply because there were so many in the past century, because memories are not transmitted like genes. Humans have minds but are not intelligent enough to learn from the past, and when malevolence flares up in the human mind it can endanger human survival itself.

The human species does not necessarily move in stages from progress to progress, and here I make reference to the history of human civilisation. History and civilisation do not advance in tandem. From the stagnation of Medieval Europe to the decline and chaos in recent times on the mainland of Asia and to the catastrophes of two world wars in the twentieth century, the methods of killing people became increasingly sophisticated. Scientific and technological progress certainly does not imply that humankind as a result becomes more civilised.

Using some scientific -ism to explain history or interpreting it with a historical perspective based on pseudo-dialectics have failed to clarify human behaviour. Now that the utopian fervour and continuing revolution of the past century have crumbled to dust, there is unavoidably a feeling of bitterness amongst those who have survived.

The denial of a denial does not necessarily result in an affirmation. Revolution did not merely bring in new things because the new utopian world was premised on the destruction of the old. This theory of social revolution was similarly applied to literature and turned what had once been a realm of creativity into a battlefield in which earlier people were overthrown and cultural traditions were trampled upon. Everything had to start from zero, modernisation was good, and the history of literature too was interpreted as a continuing upheaval.

The writer cannot fill the role of the Creator so there is no need for him to inflate his ego by thinking that he is God. This will not only bring about psychological dysfunction and turn him into a madman but will also transform the world into a hallucination in which everything external to his own body is purgatory and naturally he cannot go on living. Others are clearly hell: presumably it is like this when the self loses control. Needless to say he will turn himself into a sacrifice for the future and also demand that others follow suit in sacrificing themselves.

There is no need to rush to complete the history of the twentieth century. If the world again sinks into the ruins of some ideological framework this history will have been written in vain and later people will revise it for themselves.

The writer is also not a prophet. What is important is to live in the present, to stop being hoodwinked, to cast off delusions, to look clearly at this moment of time and at the same time to scrutinise the self. This self too is total chaos, and while questioning the world and others one may as well look back at one's self. Disaster and oppression do usually come from another, but man's cowardice and anxiety can often intensify the suffering and furthermore create misfortune for others.

Such is the inexplicable nature of humankind's behaviour, and man's knowledge of his self is even harder to comprehend. Literature is simply man focusing his gaze on his self and while he does a thread of consciousness which sheds light on this self begins to grow.

To subvert is not the aim of literature; its value lies in discovering and revealing what is rarely known, little known, thought to be known but in fact not very well known of the truth of the human world. It would seem that truth is the unassailable and most basic quality of literature.

The new century has already arrived. I will not bother about whether or not it is in fact new but it would seem that the revolution in literature and revolutionary literature, and even ideology, may have all come to an end. The illusion of a social utopia that enshrouded more than a century has vanished and when literature throws off the fetters of this and that -ism it will still have to return to the dilemmas of human existence. However, the dilemmas of human existence have changed very little and will continue to be the eternal topic of literature.

This is an age without prophecies and promises, and I think it is a good thing. The writer playing prophet and judge should also cease since the many prophecies of the past century have all turned out to be frauds. And there is no need to manufacture new superstitions about the future; it is much better to wait and see. It would be best also for the writer to revert to the role of witness and strive to present the truth.

This is not to say that literature is the same as a document. Actually, there are few facts in documented testimonies, and the reasons and motives behind incidents are often concealed. However, when literature deals with the truth the whole process from a person's inner mind to the incident can be exposed without leaving anything out. This power is inherent in literature as long as the writer sets out to portray the true circumstances of human existence and is not just making up nonsense.

It is a writer's insights in grasping truth that determine the quality of a work, and word games or writing techniques cannot serve as substitutes. Indeed, there are numerous definitions of truth and how it is dealt with varies from person to person, but it can be seen at a glance whether a writer is embellishing human phenomena or making a full and honest portrayal. The literary criticism of a certain ideology turned truth and untruth into semantic analysis, but such principles and tenets are of little relevance in literary creation.

However, whether or not the writer confronts truth is not just an issue of creative methodology, it is closely linked to his attitude towards writing. Truth in writing implies sincerity when the pen is put down. Here truth is not simply an evaluation of literature but at the same time has ethical connotations. It is not the writer's duty to preach morality and while striving to portray various people in the world he also unscrupulously exposes his self, even the secrets of his inner mind. For the writer truth in literature approximates ethics; it is the ultimate ethics of literature.

In the hands of a writer with a serious attitude to writing, even literary fabrications are premised on the portrayal of the truth of human life, and this has been the vital life force of works that have endured from ancient times to the present. It is precisely for this reason that Greek tragedy and Shakespeare will never become outdated.

Literature does not simply make a replica of reality but penetrates the surface layers and reaches deep into the inner workings of reality; it removes false illusions, looks down from great heights at ordinary happenings and, with a broad perspective, reveals happenings in their entirety.

Of course literature also relies on the imagination, but this sort of journey in the mind is not just putting together a whole lot of rubbish. Imagination that is divorced from true feelings and fabrications that are divorced from the basis of life experiences can only end up insipid and weak, and works that fail to convince the author himself will not be able to move readers. Indeed, literature does not only rely on the experiences of ordinary life nor is the writer bound by what he has personally experienced. It is possible for the things heard and seen through a language carrier and the things related in the literary works of earlier writers all to be transformed into one's own feelings. This too is the magic of the language of literature.

As with a curse or a blessing language has the power to stir body and mind. The art of language lies in the presenter being able to convey his feelings to others; it is not some sign system or semantic structure requiring nothing more than grammatical structures. If the living person behind language is forgotten, semantic expositions easily turn into games of the intellect.

Language is not merely concepts and the carrier of concepts; it simultaneously activates the feelings and the senses, and this is why signs and signals cannot replace the language of living people. The will, motives, tone and emotions behind what someone says cannot be fully expressed by semantics and rhetoric alone. The connotations of the language of literature must be voiced, spoken by living people, to be fully expressed. So as well as serving as a carrier of thought, literature must also appeal to the auditory senses. The human need for language is not simply for the transmission of meaning; it is at the same time listening to and affirming a person's existence.

Borrowing from Descartes, it could be said of the writer: I say and therefore I am. However, the I of the writer can be the writer himself, can be equated to the narrator, or become the characters of a work. As the narrator-subject can also be he and you, it is tripartite. The fixing of a key-speaker pronoun is the starting point for portraying perceptions and from this various narrative patterns take shape. It is during the process of searching for his own narrative method that the writer gives concrete form to his perceptions.

In my fiction I use pronouns instead of the usual characters and also use the pronouns I, you, and he to tell about or to focus on the protagonist. The portrayal of the one character by using different pronouns creates a sense of distance. As this also provides actors on the stage with a broader psychological space I have also introduced the changing of pronouns into my drama.

The writing of fiction or drama has not and will not come to an end and there is no substance to flippant announcements of the death of certain genres of literature or art.

Born at the start of human civilisation language, like life, is full of wonders, and its expressive capacity is limitless. It is the work of the writer to discover and develop the latent potential inherent in language. The writer is not the Creator and he cannot eradicate the world even if it is too old. He also cannot establish some new ideal world even if the present world is absurd and beyond human comprehension. However, he can certainly make innovative statements either by adding to what earlier people have said or else starting where earlier people stopped.

To subvert literature was Cultural Revolution rhetoric. Literature did not die and writers were not destroyed. Every writer has his place on the bookshelf, and he has life as long as he has readers. There is no greater consolation for a writer than to be able to leave a book in humankind's vast treasury of literature that will continue to be read in future times.

Literature is only actualised and of interest at that moment in time when the writer writes it and the reader reads it. Unless it is pretence, to write for the future only deludes oneself and others as well. Literature is for the living and moreover affirms the present of the living. It is this eternal present and this confirmation of individual life that is the absolute reason why literature is literature, if one insists on seeking a reason for this huge thing that exists of itself.

When writing is not a livelihood or when one is so engrossed in writing that one forgets why one is writing and for whom one is writing, it becomes a necessity and one will write compulsively and give birth to literature. It is this non-utilitarian aspect of literature that is fundamental to literature. That the writing of literature has become a profession is an ugly outcome of the division of labour in modern society and a very bitter fruit for the writer.

This is especially the case in the present age where the market economy has become pervasive and books have also become commodities. Everywhere there are huge undiscriminating markets, and not just individual writers but even the societies and movements of past literary schools have all gone. If the writer does not bend to the pressures of the market and refuses to stoop to manufacturing cultural products by writing to satisfy the tastes of fashions and trends, he must make a living by some other means. Literature is not a best-selling book or a book on a ranked list, and authors promoted on television are engaged in advertising rather than in writing. Freedom in writing is not conferred and cannot be purchased but comes from an inner need in the writer himself.

Instead of saying that Buddha is in the heart it would be better to say that freedom is in the heart, and it simply depends on whether one makes use of it. If one exchanges freedom for something else, then the bird that is freedom will fly off, for this is the cost of freedom.

The writer writes what he wants without concern for recompense not only to affirm his self but also to challenge society. This challenge is not pretence and the writer has no need to inflate his ego by becoming a hero or a fighter. Heroes and fighters struggle to achieve some great work or to establish some meritorious deed, and these lie beyond the scope of literary works. If the writer wants to challenge society it must be through language, and he must rely on the characters and incidents of his works, otherwise he can only harm literature. Literature is not angry shouting and furthermore cannot turn an individual's indignation into accusations. It is only when the feelings of the writer as an individual are dispersed in a work that his feelings will withstand the ravages of time and live on for a long time.

Therefore it is actually not the challenge of the writer to society but rather the challenge of his works. An enduring work is of course a powerful response to the times and society of the writer. The clamour of the writer and his actions may have vanished, but as long as there are readers his voice in his writings continues to reverberate.

Indeed such a challenge cannot transform society. It is merely an individual aspiring to transcend the limitations of the social ecology and taking a very inconspicuous stance. However, this is by no means an ordinary stance for it is one that takes pride in being human. It would be sad if human history is only manipulated by the unknowable laws and moves blindly with the current so that the different voices of individuals cannot be heard. It is in this sense that literature fills in the gaps of history. When the great laws of history are not used to explain humankind it will be possible for people to leave behind their own voices. History is not all that humankind possesses: there is also the legacy of literature. In literature the people are inventions, but they retain an essential belief in their own self-worth.

Honourable members of the Academy, I thank you for awarding this Nobel Prize to literature, to literature that is unwavering in its independence, that avoids neither human suffering nor political oppression and that, furthermore, does not serve politics. I thank all of you for awarding this most prestigious prize for works that are far removed from the writings of the market, works that have aroused little attention but are actually worth reading. At the same time, I also thank the Swedish Academy for allowing me to ascend this dais to speak before the eyes of the world. A frail individual's weak voice that is hardly worth listening to and that normally would not be heard in the public media has been allowed to address the world. However, I believe that this is precisely the meaning of the Nobel Prize and I thank everyone for this opportunity to speak.

*Translated by Mabel Lee*